Early Learning Center Games

41 "Easy-to-Make" and "Fun-to-Play" Skill Building Games

by

Marilee Woodfield

Publisher

Key Education Publishing Company, LLC

Minneapolis, Minnesota

CONGRATULATIONS ON YOUR PURCHASE OF A KEY EDUCATION PRODUCT!

The editors at Key Education are former teachers who bring experience, enthusiasm, and quality to each and every product. Thousands of teachers have looked to the staff at Key Education for new and innovative resources to make their work more enjoyable and rewarding. Key Education is committed to developing and publishing educational materials that will assist teachers in building a strong and developmentally appropriate curriculum for young children.

PLAN FOR GREAT TEACHING EXPERIENCES WHEN YOU USE EDUCATIONAL MATERIALS FROM KEY EDUCATION PUBLISHING COMPANY, LLC!

Credits

Author: Marilee Woodfield
Publisher: Sherrill B. Flora
Editors: Kelly Huxmann, George C. Flora
Inside Illustrations: Marilee Woodfield
　　　　　　　　　　　　Julie Anderson
　　　　　　　　　　　　Janet Armbrust
　　　　　　　　　　　　Vanessa Countryman
　　　　　　　　　　　　Katie Flora
Page Design and Layout: Kelly Huxmann
Creative Director: Annette-Hollister-Papp

Key Education welcomes manuscripts and product ideas from teachers. For a copy of our submission guidelines, please send a self-addressed, stamped envelope to:

Key Education Publishing Company, LLC
Acquisitions Department
9601 Newton Avenue South
Minneapolis, Minnesota 55431

About the Author

In addition to teaching and directing preschools for 20 years, Marilee Woodfield graduated with a with a BS in Human Development from Brigham Young University. In addition to writing teacher resource books, Marilee spends her time teaching preschool music, driving the family taxi service and engaging in various home-improvement projects. Marilee currently resides in Texas with her husband and 4 children.

Copyright Notice

Standard Book Number: 1-933052-27-9
Early Learning Center Games
Copyright © 2006 by Key Education Publishing Company, LLC
Minneapolis, Minnesota 55431

Table of Contents

Skills Reference Table

Introduction

Got five minutes? How about ten or fifteen? File folders are a handy resource for making the most of small moments during the day. In addition to giving busy hands something to do, file folder games are great for exercising small motor skills; for developing sorting, matching, and other critical thinking skills; as well as for building color, number, letter, and shape recognition.

While every file folder game develops fine motor skills, here are a few other skills that children will strengthen while playing with these file folder games:

- Following step-by-step instructions
- Phonological awareness
- Print awareness
- Early writing skills
- Alphabet knowledge
- Number recognition
- Geometry and spatial sense

- Patterning
- Scientific knowledge
- Give-and-take in social interactions
- Making independent choices
- Persisting in activities
- Increasing concentration
- Finding more than one solution

Along with a few simple supplies, *Early Learning Center Games* provides everything you need to create fun learning experiences for your children. Use the file folders to focus on a specific theme or to work on a particular skill, such as one-to-one correspondence or color recognition. The Skills Reference Table on page 3 will help you locate just the right file folder game.

Basic Assembly Tips

While each file folder game is unique, here are some general assembly tips that will prove helpful as you create your own collection of file folder games:

Copying — Each set of game instructions describes how many copies of each pattern are needed. Be sure to use high-quality paper for all copies, and use heavy card stock for any item that will be handled by the children. The items will be easier to manipulate and will last longer, too. If the pattern you are using does not have specific coloring instructions, consider copying onto colorful or patterned papers to help cut down on your preparation time.

Coloring — Although it may seem daunting to color each little piece, take the time to make each file folder colorful and inviting. After all, if you prepare it correctly, you will be able to use each file folder game for a long time.

Cutting — Careful cutting will result in a more professional-looking product. When trimming lamination on card stock or the file folders themselves, leave a 1/8" margin around the outside edges. If you trim too closely, the lamination will be prone to separate and peel apart.

Laminating — Although it may seem that you go through miles and miles of lamination, it is absolutely necessary to protect your file folder games. Be sure to laminate all of the pieces before you offer them to busy little hands.

Pockets and Windows — Several of the games use pockets or windows for play. A **pocket** is a hole or cavity in the file folder into which game pieces can be inserted (e.g., a train car with a pocket for loading cargo). To make a pocket, glue only along the bottom and side edges of an object when attaching it to the file folder. After the folder has been laminated, create the pocket by carefully cutting a slit along the top of the object with **a craft knife.** A window is essentially a see-through pocket. To create a window, begin by cutting out the middle of an object as indicated (e.g., the center of a fishbowl) and laminate the individual piece. Then attach the piece to the file folder and laminate the entire folder. Cut a slit along the top of the piece to create an opening where objects can be slid into the pocket and seen through the window.

Sticky Tack vs. Velcro® — Sticky-tack adhesive is suggested as a way to apply pieces in several of the file folder games, but you can use whatever works best for you. If you use sticky tack, you won't have to reassemble a file folder whenever the Velcro tabs get pulled off. And without the Velcro tabs providing a hint, children will have to think before sticking an object in the folder. For example, if an activity calls for putting five buttons on a snowperson, a child using sticky tack must actually count out the five buttons. A child using Velcro might just stick five buttons on the snowperson without counting, simply because there were five Velcro tabs on the folder.

Storage and Labeling — Label everything. Use the file folder name tags provided on each game instruction page to label the file folder itself and any plastic storage bags. Give each file folder game a number as well, and write that number on the back of each game piece. This way when pieces from two or more games get mixed up, putting them back in the right place will be a snap. Store all of the extra pieces for games in plastic zippered bags. Staple each bag to the file folder so that everything you need to complete the activity is always with the folder.

Organizing — One simple idea for organizing your file folders is to color-code them. Use yellow for activities that develop literacy skills, purple for number operations, and so on.

File Folders — Using a colorful file folder will perk up a game's personality. Glue the file folder name tag onto the tab to identify each game. Then add the directions for how to play the game and any other decorations desired on the outside of the file folder. For example, when creating the "Birds on a Wire" file folder, make an additional copy of the bird patterns page and add a few birds to the front of the folder.

Extending Your File Folder Experiences

- Make multiple copies of the same file folder so that more than one child can play at a time.
- As the children's skill levels increase, adjust the difficulty of the file folder concepts. For example, use higher numbers for counting or more difficult patterning sequences.
- Make copies of the pattern pages to use for individual activities.

Alphabet Zoo

Theme: Alphabet, Animals, Zoo

Skills: Sorting, Beginning sounds

Preparation:

1. Make four copies of the zoo cage pattern (page 7). Cut out along the dashed lines and cut out the spaces between the cage bars. Laminate each cage separately and trim around the outside edges only.

2. Make one copy of the animal patterns (pages 7–9). Color the animals as desired and cut out along the dashed lines. Laminate each animal separately and trim.

Assembly:

1. Using clear tape, tape the four laminated cages to the inside of a file folder as shown above. Tape only along the bottom and side edges of each cage, leaving the top free.

2. Place a file folder name tag and the "To Play" instruction box on the outside of the file folder as shown on page 5.

3. Laminate the entire file folder. Trim around the edges.

4. Use a craft knife to make window pockets. Carefully cut a slit through the laminate along the top edge of each cage. Be sure not to cut through the file folder itself.

5. Place all of the animals in a quart-sized plastic zippered bag. Label the bag with a name tag and attach to the front of the file folder.

Extension:

Extend the play by laminating additional pictures of other zoo animals.

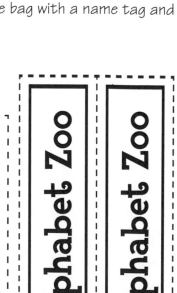

To Play:

- Sort the animals by the beginning letter sounds of their names. Use a separate cage for each sound.

- Use a washable or a dry-erase marker to write the beginning letter of each animal's name in the small box on the cage.

- Once all of the cages are filled, erase the letters in the boxes and put new animals in the cages.

Alphabet Zoo

cut out   cut out   cut out   cut out

Bear

Lion

Alphabet Zoo

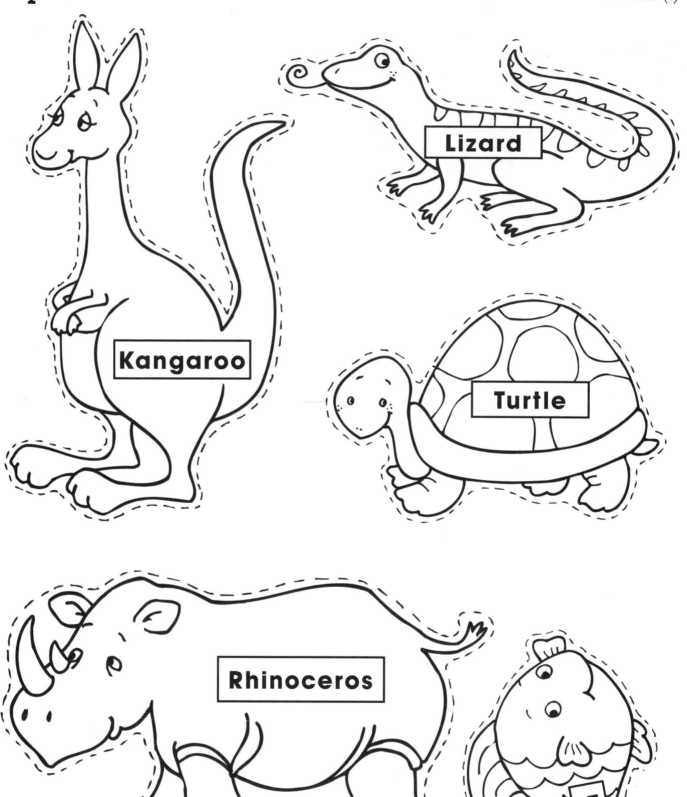

Kangaroo

Lizard

Turtle

Rhinoceros

Fish

TOY BOX

Theme: Toys

Skills: Ending sounds, Sorting

Preparation:

1. Make six copies of the toy box pattern (page 11). Color as desired. Write the letters **g, l, n, r, s,** and **t** on the fronts of the boxes, using a different letter for each box. Cut out along the dashed lines. Laminate each toy box separately and trim.

2. Make one copy of the toy patterns (pages 11–12). Color the toys as desired. Cut out along the dashed lines. Laminate each toy separately and trim.

Assembly:

1. Glue the laminated toy boxes to the inside of a file folder as shown here. Glue only along the outside edges of each toy box, leaving the center free of glue.

2. Attach a file folder name tag and the "To Play" instruction box on the outside of the file folder as shown on page 5.

3. Laminate the entire file folder. Trim around the edges.

4. Use a craft knife to cut pockets in the toy boxes. Carefully cut a slit along the dashed line across the top of each toy box. Be sure not to cut through the file folder itself.

5. Place all of the toys in a quart-sized plastic zippered bag. Label the bag with a name tag and attach to the front of the file folder.

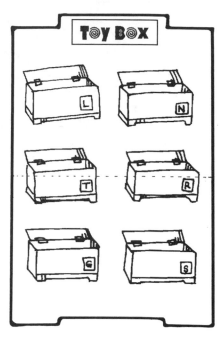

Extension:

Extend the play by laminating several index cards with familiar words written on them. Have the children sort the words into the toy boxes according to their ending sounds.

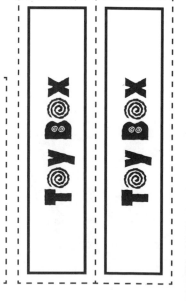

To Play:

- Look at the letter on each toy box.
- Fill each box with a picture of an object that ends in the sound indicated by the letter. (For example, put the ball in the box labeled with the letter **l**.)

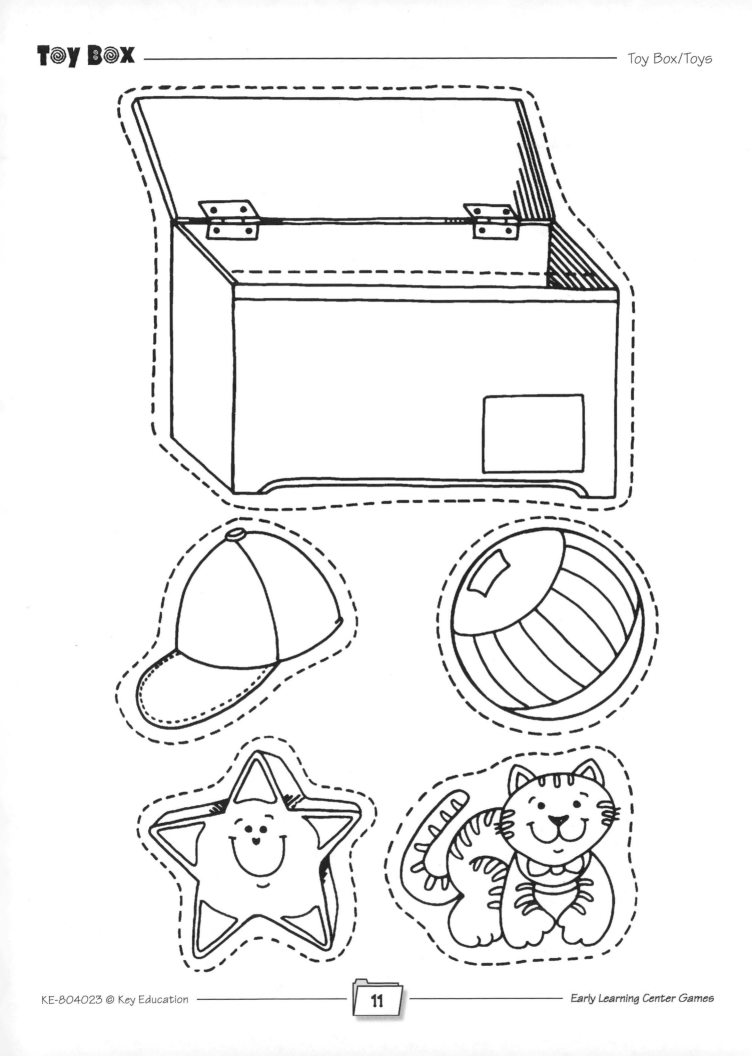

Astronauts and Aliens

Theme: Space

Skill: Rhyming words

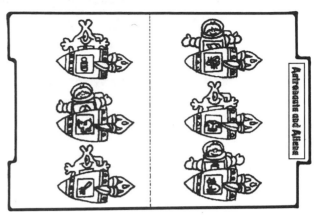

Preparation:

1. Make one copy of the spaceship patterns (page 14). Color as desired. Cut out the spaceships along the dashed lines. Laminate each ship separately and trim.

2. Make one copy of both the astronauts and aliens patterns (pages 15–16). Color as desired. Cut out the figures along the dashed lines. Laminate each figure separately and trim.

Assembly:

1. Glue the laminated spaceships to the inside of a file folder as shown above. Glue only along the outside edges of each spaceship, leaving the center free of glue.

2. Attach a file folder name tag and the "To Play" instruction box on the outside of the file folder as shown on page 5.

3. Laminate the entire file folder. Trim around the edges.

4. Use a craft knife to create pockets. Carefully cut a slit through the laminate along the dashed line on each spaceship. Be sure not to cut through the file folder itself.

5. Place all of the astronauts and aliens in a quart-sized plastic zippered bag. Label the bag with a name tag and attach to the front of the file folder.

To Play:

- Look at the picture on each spaceship. Think of the name for the object.

- Find the astronaut or alien with a picture whose name rhymes with the first picture and place it in the matching spaceship.

Astronauts and Aliens

Astronauts and Aliens

Astronauts and Aliens

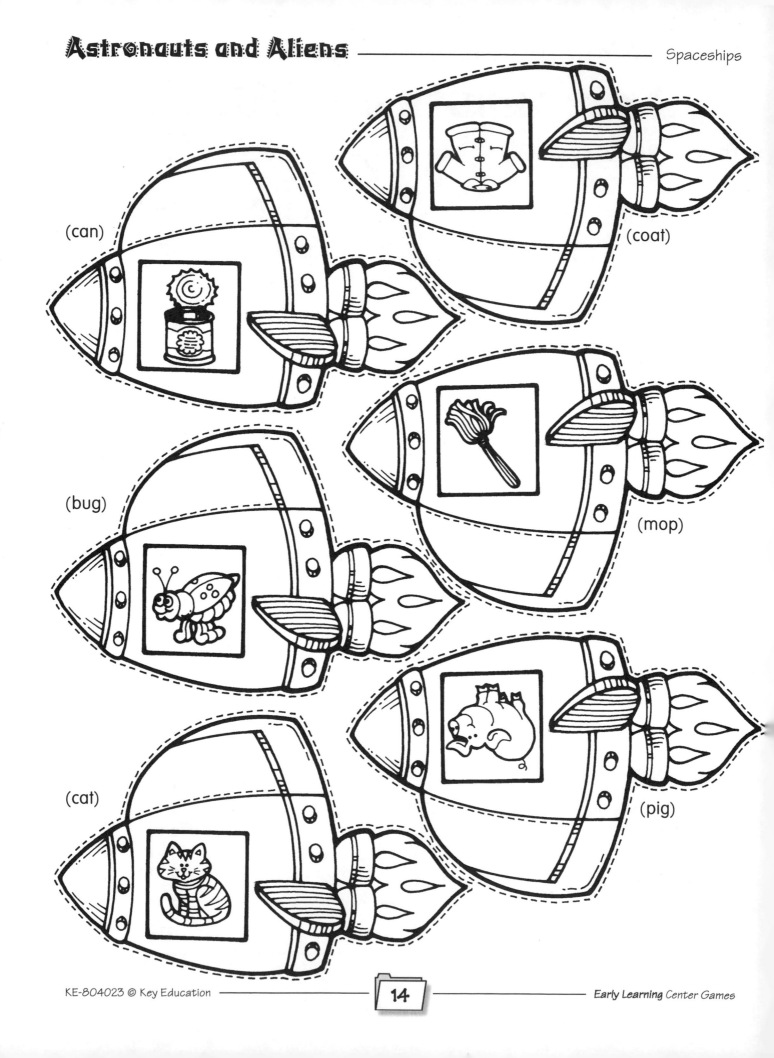

(can)

(coat)

(bug)

(mop)

(cat)

(pig)

14

(wig)

(hat)

(man)

(goat)

(top)

(rug)

(stop)

(bat)

(boat)

(dig)

(mug)

(pan)

Twinkle Little Star

Theme: Space

Skills: Matching, Number recognition, Number words, Sets

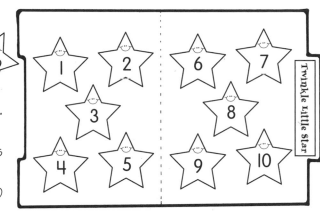

Preparation:

1. Make eight copies of the star patterns (page 18). Color as desired.
2. Write the numerals 1–10 on two sets of 10 stars each, one number per star.
3. Write the number words **one** through **ten** on 10 more stars, one word per star.
4. Draw dots to correspond with the numbers 1–10 on the last 10 stars. For example, draw one dot on the first star, two dots on the second star, etc.
5. Cut out the stars along the dashed lines. Laminate each star separately and trim.

Assembly:

1. Glue one set of the numbered stars (from step 2 above) to the inside of a file folder as shown above.
2. Attach a file folder name tag and the "To Play" instruction box on the outside of the file folder as shown on page 5.
3. Laminate the entire file folder. Trim around the edges.
4. Place the laminated stars with numerals, number words, and dots in three separate plastic zippered sandwich bags. Label each bag with a name tag and attach to the front of the file folder.

Extension:

Expand this activity by including the numbers 11–20, or by creating another set of stars with simple math sentences that have answers 1–10.

To Play:

- Look at each star on the inside of the file folder.
- Find another star with the matching numeral, number word, or dot set and place it on top of the first star.

Twinkle Little Star

Twinkle Little Star

Twinkle Little Star

18

Shape Match

Theme: Shapes

Skills: Shapes, Sorting, Counting, Matching

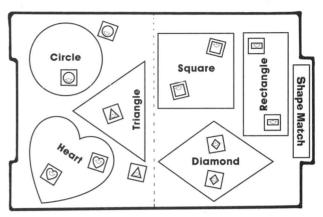

Preparation:

1. Make one copy of all the large shape patterns (pages 20–21). Color as desired and cut out the shapes along the dashed lines.

2. Make four copies of the small shape patterns (page 22) on colorful paper. Cut apart the shapes along the dashed lines. Laminate each piece separately and trim.

Assembly:

1. Glue the large shapes to the inside of a file folder as shown above.

2. Attach the file folder name tag and the "To Play" instruction box on the outside of the file folder as shown on page 5.

3. Laminate the entire file folder. Trim around the edges.

4. Place the small, cutout shapes and one die in a quart-sized plastic zippered bag. Label the bag with a name tag and attach to the front of the file folder.

To Play:

- Draw one small shape from the bag.
- Roll the die.
- Take the same number of small shapes as the number rolled on the die. Then place them on the matching large shape on the file folder. (For example, if you draw a heart and roll a 3, take three small heart shapes and place them on the large heart shape in the file folder.)
- Continue rolling and placing the shapes until they are all gone.

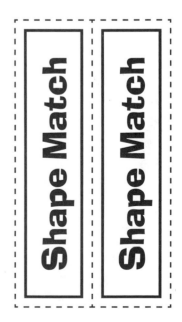

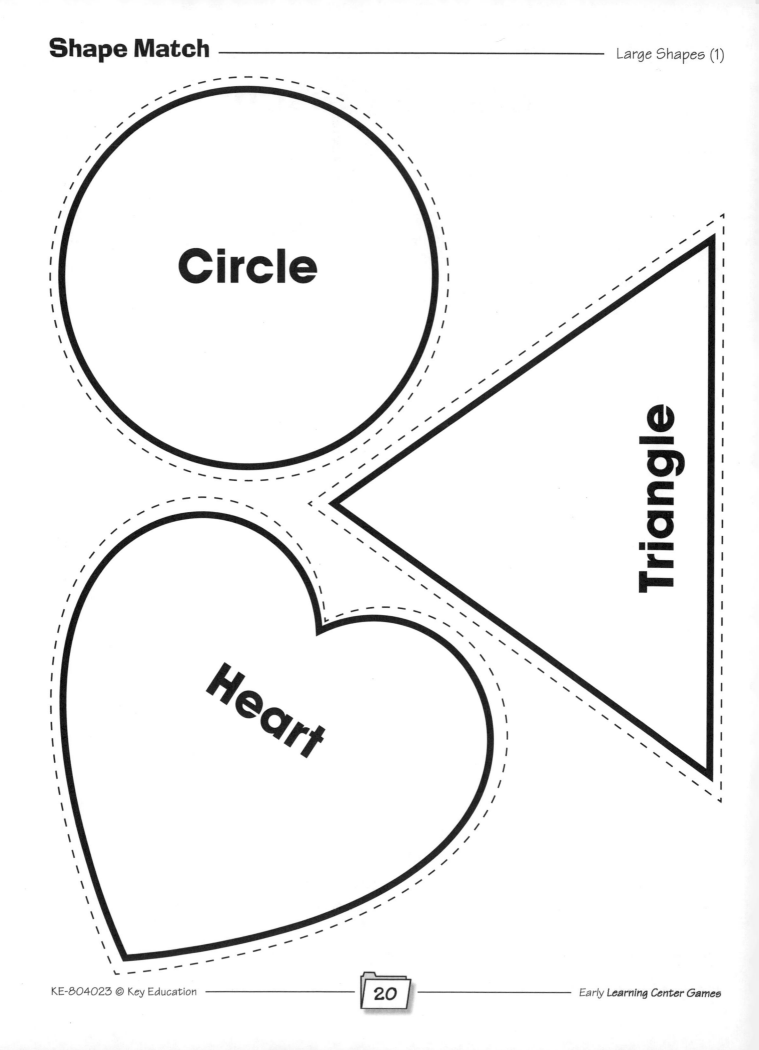

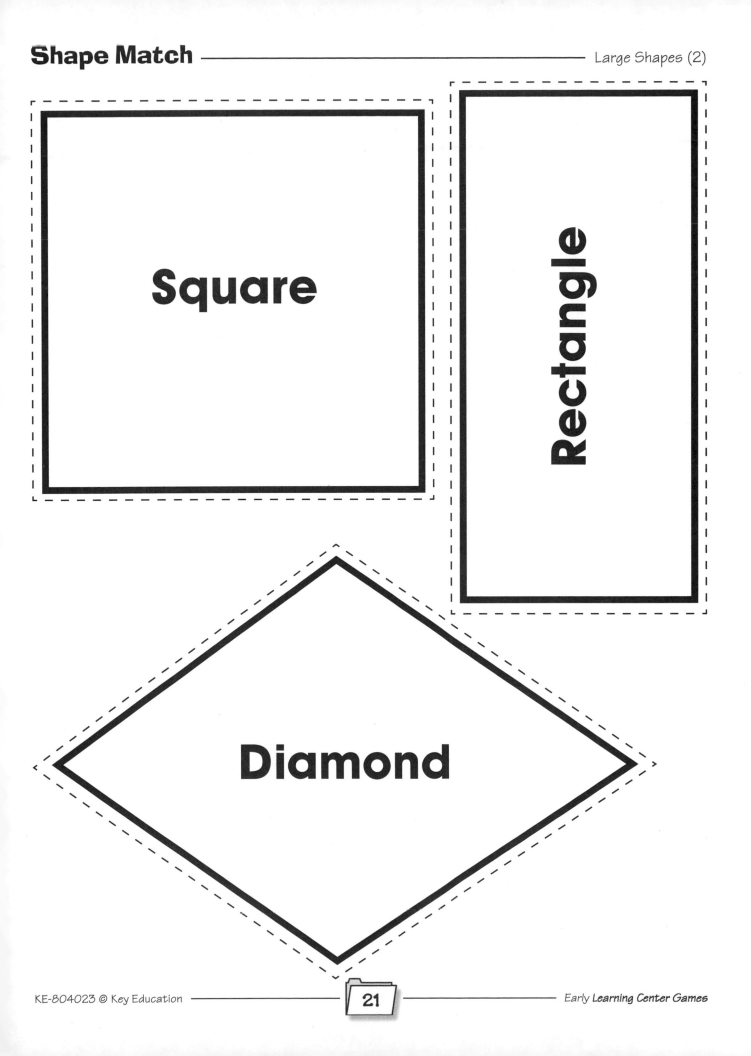

Square

Rectangle

Diamond

Shape Match

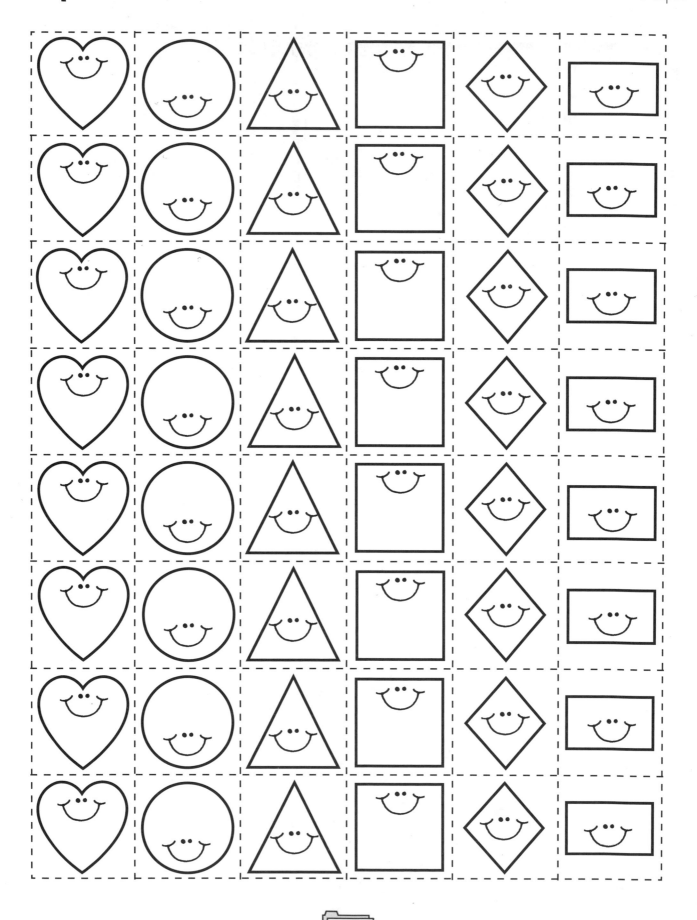

Word Bugs

Theme: Insects

Skills: Letter recognition, Pre-reading skills

Preparation:

1. Make at least six copies of the bug body parts patterns (page 24) on colorful paper. Cut out the pieces along the dashed lines. Set aside the bug heads for now.

2. Write the letters of the alphabet on the bug body segments, one letter per segment. Laminate each piece separately and trim.

3. Make one copy of the word cards (page 25) on heavy card stock. Cut apart along the dashed lines. Color if desired. Laminate each card separately and trim.

Assembly:

1. Glue the bug heads to the inside of a file folder as shown above.

2. Attach the file folder name tag and the "To Play" instruction box on the outside of the file folder as shown on page 5.

3. Laminate the entire file folder. Trim around the edges.

4. Place the word cards and the bug body parts in two separate plastic zippered sandwich bags. Label the bags with name tags and attach them to the front of the file folder.

5. Place a small ball of sticky-tack adhesive in a snack-sized zippered bag and staple to the front of the other bags. Alternatively, add Velcro tabs to the file folder and to the backs of the bug pieces.

Extension:

Create additional word cards using the children's names or words from the childrens' vocabulary lists.

To Play:

- Select a card from the bag of word cards.
- Create a word bug by sticking the lettered bug body parts in order to match the letters on the word card.

apple	**ball**	**boat**	**candy**
cat	**chair**	**dad**	**dog**
door	**fish**	**mom**	**paint**
shirt	**sock**	**table**	**top**

BUILD A STORY

Theme: Books and stories

Skills: Literacy, Pre-reading skills

Preparation:

1. Make eight copies of the book background pattern (page 27). Color the pages so that they are all identical. Cut out along the solid black lines.

2. Make eight copies of the character/scenery patterns (pages 28–30). Also color these patterns so that they are all identical. Cut out the figures along the dashed lines. Laminate each figure separately and trim.

Assembly:

1. Glue two background pages to the inside of a file folder so that the edges meet at the fold as shown above. Glue the remaining background pages back-to-back to create three two-sided sheets.

2. Attach the file folder name tag and the "To Play" instruction box on the outside of the file folder as shown on page 5.

3. Laminate the entire file folder and three two-sided background pages. Trim.

4. Lay one of the loose, two-sided pages on top of a background page that has been glued to the file folder. Use clear packing tape to secure the page edge at the fold in the folder. Flip the page over and secure the other side as well. Repeat with the other two background pages to create a book inside the file folder.

5. Place all of the character and scenery pieces in quart-sized plastic zippered bags. Add a ball of sticky-tack adhesive. Label the bags with name tags and attach to the front of the file folder.

To Play:

- Using the sticky tack, add characters or scenery to the book to create your own story. Use washable or dry-erase markers to draw other details as needed.

- Write or dictate a story about the pictures you have created in the box at the bottom of each page.

- Have your teacher read your story back to you when your book is complete.

BUILD A STORY

BUILD A STORY

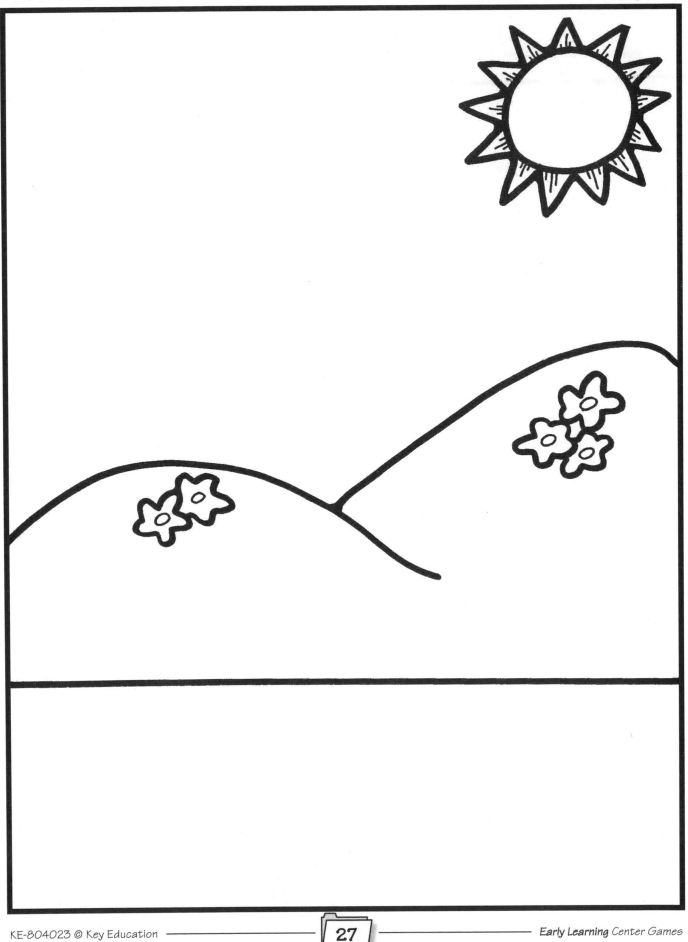

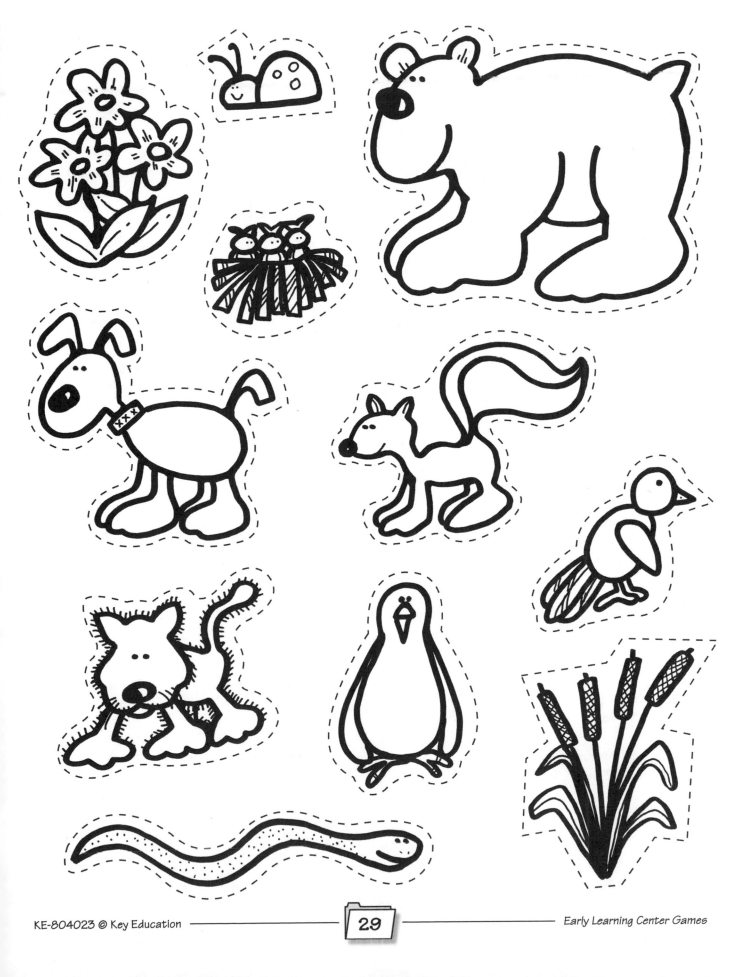

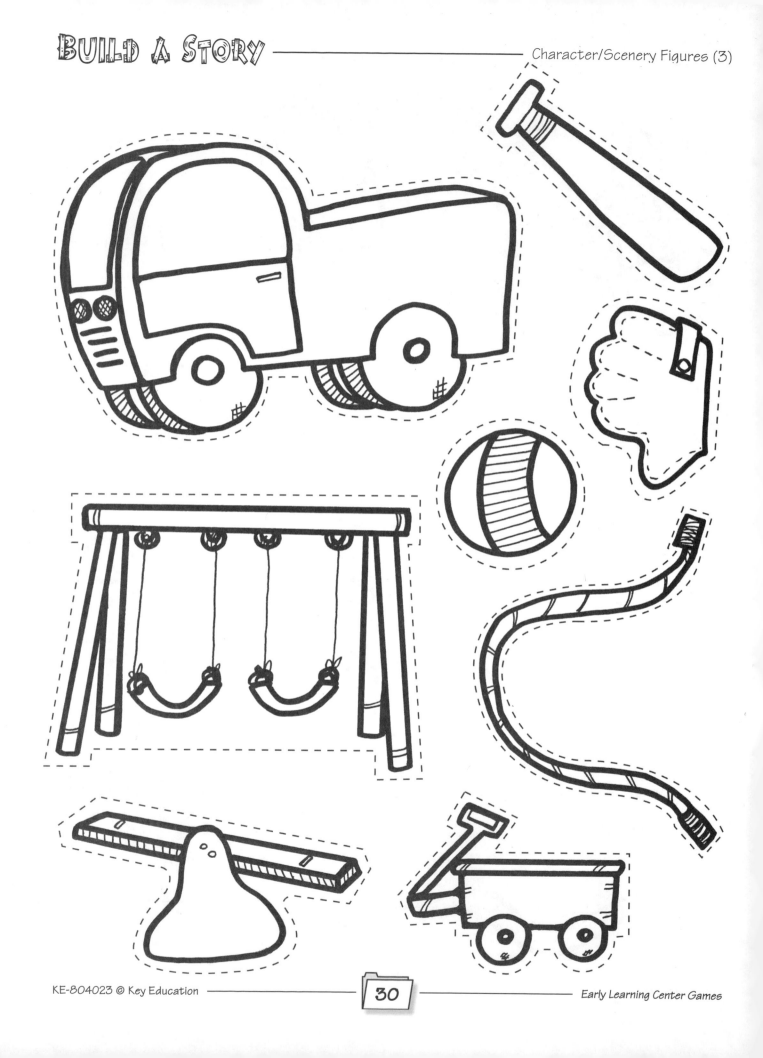

FISHBOWL

Theme: Fish

Skills: Letter recognition, Building words, Name recognition

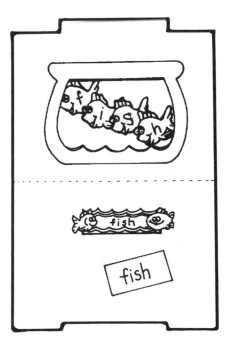

Preparation:

1. Make one copy of the fishbowl pattern (page 32). Cut out the fishbowl along the dashed line. Then cut out the inside of the bowl along the dashed line. Laminate the bowl and trim around the outside edges only.

2. Make one copy of the fish frame found on the top of page 33. Cut out along the dashed line.

3. Make several copies of the fish patterns (page 33) on colorful card stock. Write one alphabet letter on each fish. Cut out the fish along the dashed lines. Laminate each fish separately and trim.

4. Create word cards by writing the children's names and other simple words such as **dog** or **food** on 3" x 5" (7 cm x 13 cm) index cards. (See also word cards on page 25.) Laminate each card and trim.

Assembly:

1. Glue or tape the fishbowl to the inside of a file folder as shown above. Glue only along the bottom and side edges of the bowl, leaving the top free. Glue the fish frame opposite the fishbowl.

2. Attach the file folder name tag and the "To Play" instruction box on the outside of the file folder as shown on page 5.

3. Laminate the entire file folder. Trim around the edges.

4. Use a craft knife to cut a window pocket in the fishbowl. Carefully cut a slit through the laminate along the top edge of the bowl. Be sure not to cut through the file folder itself.

5. Place all of the word cards in a plastic zippered sandwich bag. Place all of the lettered fish in a quart-sized bag. Label each bag with a name tag and attach to the front of the file folder.

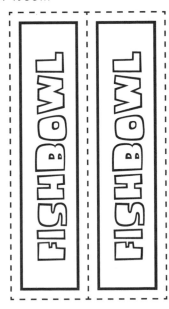

To Play:

- Select a word card from the bag.
- Find the fish with the letters in the word. Put the fish in the bowl so the letters show through the window.
- Write the word in the fish frame using a washable or dry-erase marker.
- Wipe off the word, remove the fish, and play again.

FISHBOWL

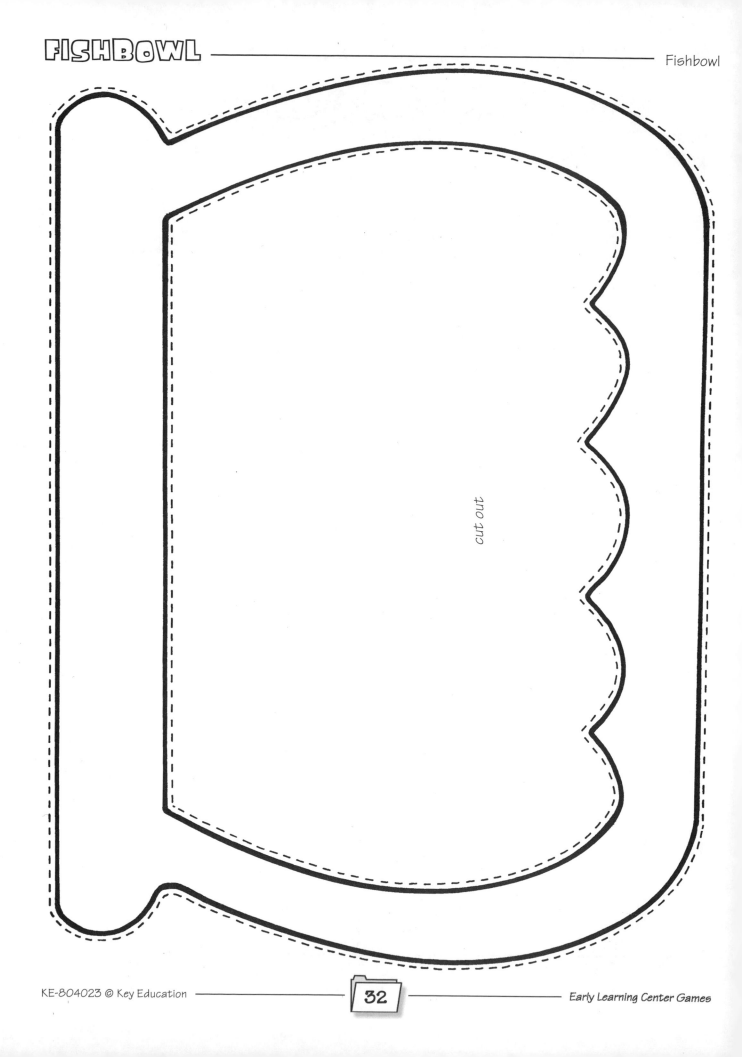

cut out

FISHBOWL

Cookie Cruncher

Theme: Food

Skill: Determining quantity

Preparation:

1. Make two copies of the cookie jar pattern (page 35). Color as desired and cut out along the dashed lines.
2. Make several copies of the cookie patterns (page 36) and color. Cut out each cookie individually, laminate, and trim.

Assembly:

1. Glue the cookie jars to the inside of a file folder on opposite sides as shown above.
2. Attach the file folder name tag and the "To Play" instruction box on the outside of the file folder as shown on page 5.
3. Laminate the entire file folder. Trim around the edges.
4. Place all of the cookies and a ball of sticky-tack adhesive in a quart-sized plastic zippered bag. Label the bag with a name tag and attach to the front of the file folder.

Extension:

Use "Cookie Cruncher" as an interactive game between partners. Create two folders, one for each child. Have each child fill the first cookie jar with cookies. Ask the children to swap folders and then have the partners put the same number of cookies in the second jar as in the first.

To Play:

- Take a handful of cookies from the bag and stick them on one cookie jar using the sticky tack.
- Count the total number of cookies. Using a washable or a dry-erase marker, write the number in the square provided on the cookie jar.
- Take the same number of cookies from the bag to fill the second cookie jar. Count to make sure you have an equal amount and write this number in the square provided on the cookie jar.

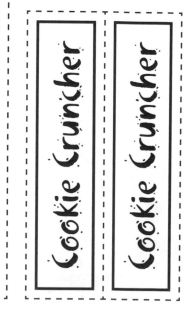

Cookies

Autobahn

Themes: Transportation, Community workers

Skills: Counting, Number recognition, Number operations

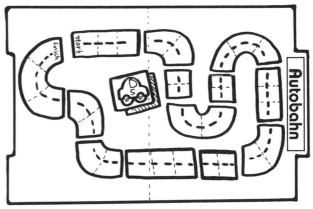

Preparation:

1. Make several copies of the road piece patterns (page 38). Cut out along the dashed lines.
2. Make several copies of the car cards (page 39) on four different colors of paper. Cut apart along the dashed lines. Set aside four cards of each color and leave them blank to use as game tokens. Write a numeral or simple math sentence on each of the remaining car cards. Laminate each card separately and trim.

Assembly:

1. Glue any combination of road pieces to the inside of a file folder, creating a continuous track as shown above. Leave a small space between the first and last pieces of track and label them "START" and "FINISH."
2. Attach the file folder name tag and the "To Play" instruction box on the outside of the file folder as shown on page 5.
3. Laminate the entire file folder. Trim around the edges.
4. Place the game token cards and the other car cards in two separate plastic zippered sandwich bags. Label each bag with a name tag and attach to the front of the file folder.

Variations:

A—Tape additional sheets to the file folder before creating the track. Laminate with the folder as one piece, then trim and fold the track to fit inside the folder.

B—Laminate all of the road pieces separately. Have the children create their own autobahn by taping the pieces end-to-end on the floor or on a table.

To Play:
- Choose a blank car card to use as a game token. Stack the other cards upside down in a pile.
- Turn over the top card and move your car along the track the number of spaces indicated on the card.
- Players take turns drawing cards and moving around the track. The first car to reach the finish line wins.

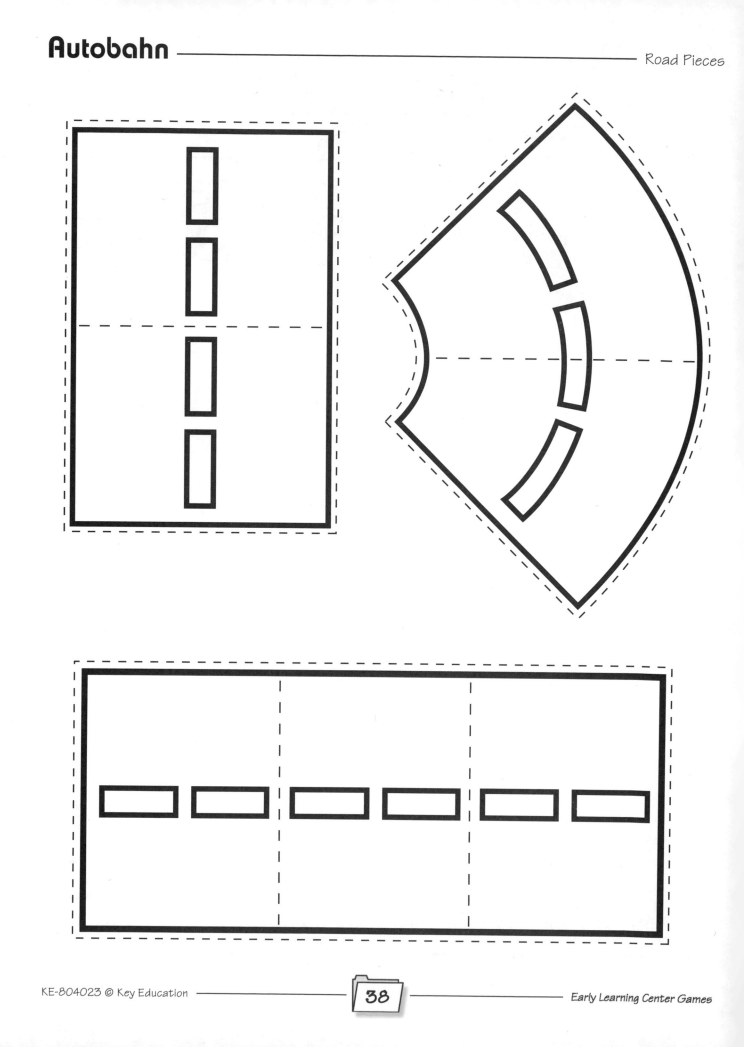

Pet Chow

Theme: Pets

Skill: One-to-one correspondence

Preparation:

1. Make two to four copies of the pet patterns (page 41). Color the pets as desired and cut out along the dashed lines.

2. Make one or two copies of the pet food patterns (page 42). Color the bowls as desired and cut out along the dashed lines. Laminate each piece separately and trim.

Assembly:

1. Glue the pets in sets of 1–4 to the inside of a file folder as shown above. Sets may be made up of different or identical pets.

2. Attach the file folder name tag and the "To Play" instruction box on the outside of the file folder as shown on page 5.

3. Laminate the entire file folder. Trim around the edges.

4. Place all of the pet food dishes in a plastic zippered sandwich bag. Add a small ball of sticky-tack adhesive to the bag. Label the bag with a name tag and attach to the front of the file folder.

To Play:

• Look at the animals inside the file folder.

• Find the bowl of pet food that is right for each animal. Stick the bowls next to the animals so that each pet has its own bowl of food.

Pet Chow

Pet Chow

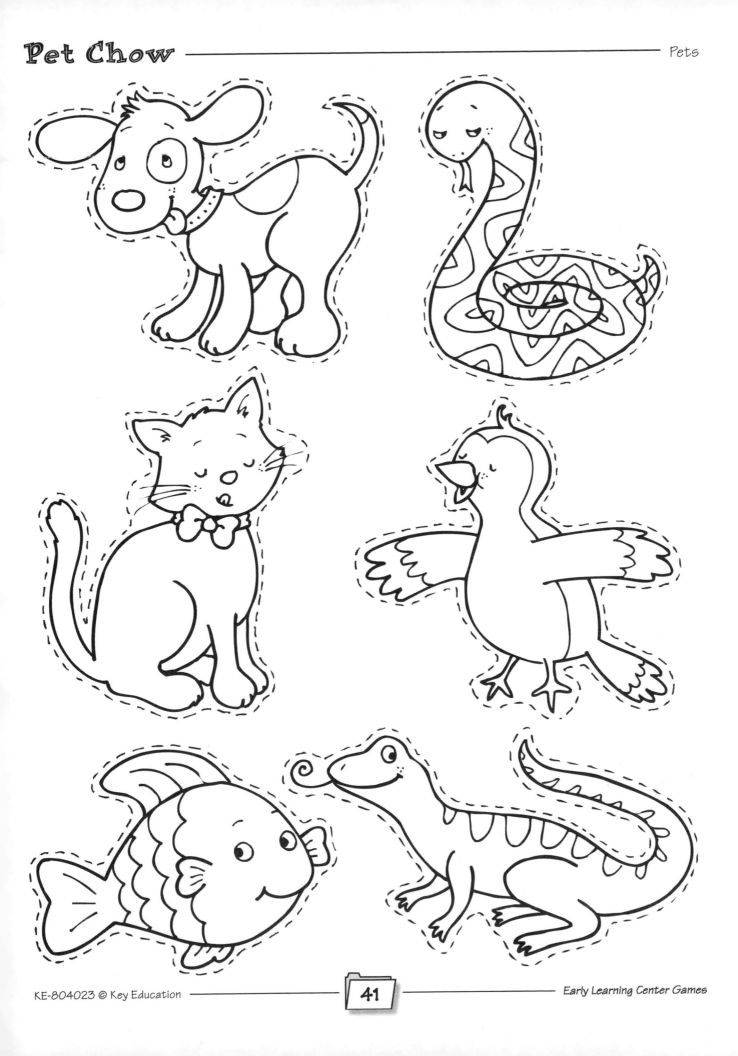

Pet Chow

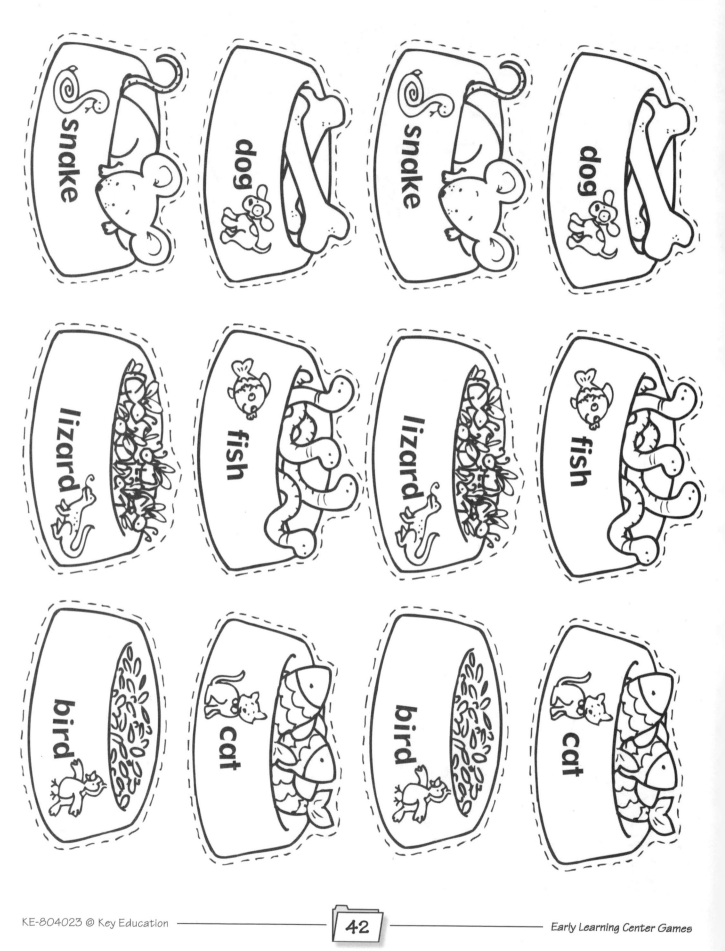

BIRDS ON A WIRE

Theme: Birds

Skill: Comparing numbers, Counting

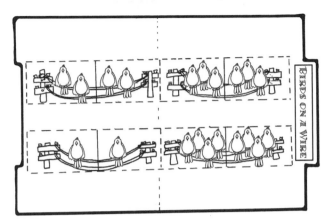

Preparation:

1. Make two copies of the telephone wire patterns (page 44). Color as desired and cut out along the dashed lines.

2. Make several copies of the bird patterns (page 45). Color the birds as desired and cut out along the dashed lines. Laminate each bird separately and trim.

Assembly:

1. Glue the four telephone wire pieces to the inside of a file folder as shown above.

2. Attach the file folder name tag and the "To Play" instruction box on the outside of the file folder as shown on page 5.

3. Laminate the entire file folder. Trim around the edges.

4. Place all of the birds and a small ball of sticky-tack adhesive in a plastic, zippered sandwich bag. Label the bag with a name tag and attach to the front of the file folder.

To Play:

- Select a few birds and stick them on the left-hand side of one telephone wire. Repeat for the other three wires.

- Go back to the first wire and add enough birds on the right-hand side of the wire to make both sides equal. Repeat for the other three wires.

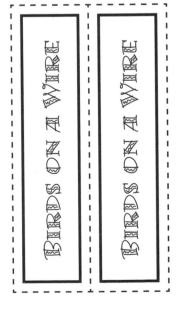

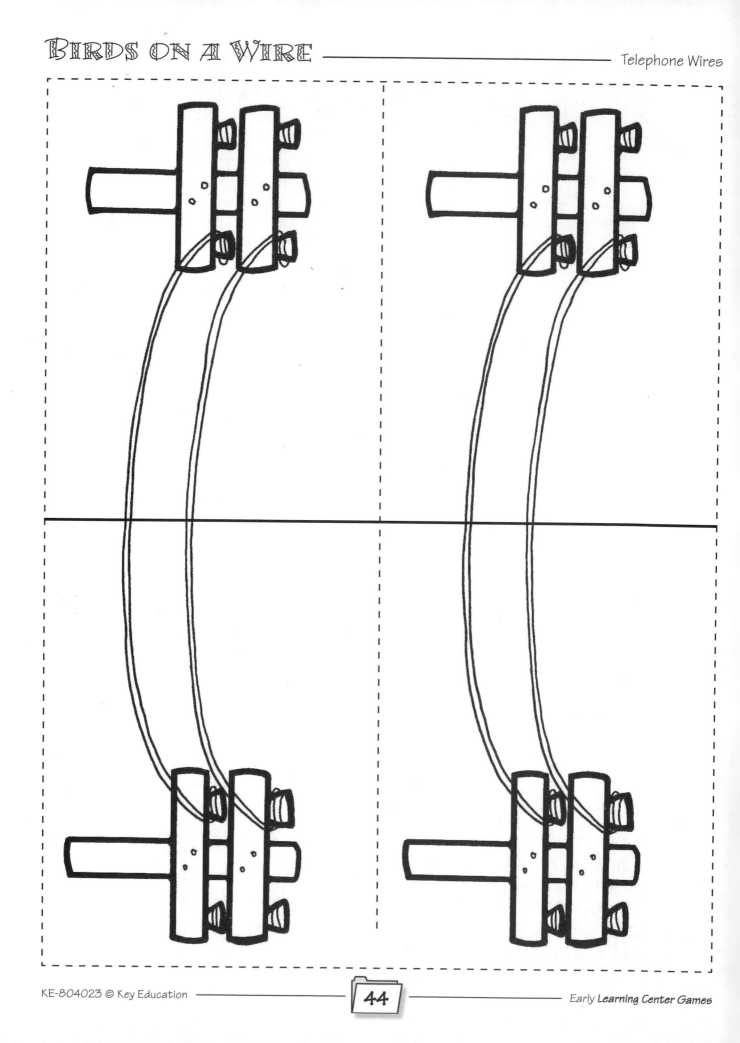

BIRDS ON A WIRE

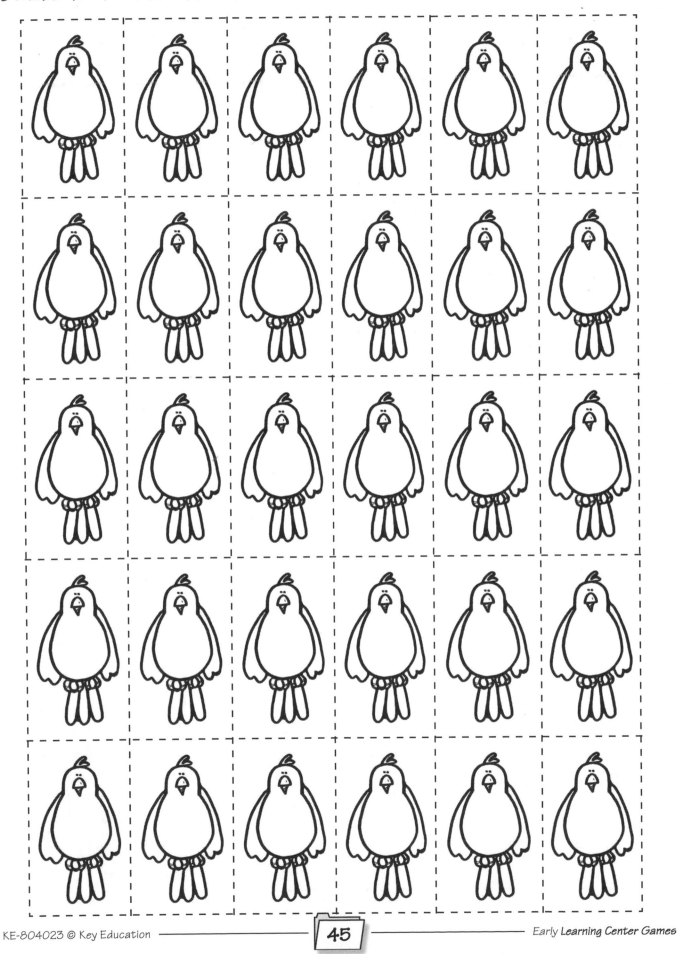

45

CRAYON BOX

Theme: Colors

Skills: Patterning, Counting, Sorting

Preparation:

1. Make three copies of the crayon box patterns (page 47). Cut out along the dashed lines. Laminate each box separately and trim.

2. Make six copies of the crayon patterns (page 48)—one copy each on red, orange, yellow, green, blue, and purple paper. Cut out the crayons along the dashed lines. Laminate each crayon separately and trim.

Assembly:

1. Glue the six crayon boxes to the inside of a file folder as shown above. Glue each box along the edges only, leaving the center free of glue.

2. Attach the file folder name tag and the "To Play" instruction box on the outside of the file folder as shown on page 5.

3. Laminate the entire file folder. Trim around the edges.

4. Use a craft knife to cut pockets. Carefully cut a slit along the dashed line at the top of each crayon box. Be sure not to cut through the file folder itself.

5. Place all of the crayons in a quart-sized plastic zippered bag. Label the bag with a name tag and attach to the front of the file folder.

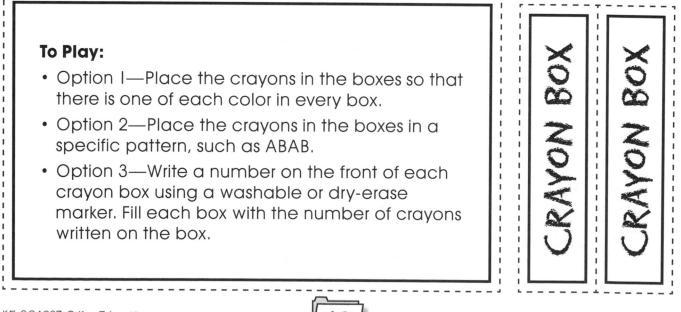

To Play:

- Option 1—Place the crayons in the boxes so that there is one of each color in every box.

- Option 2—Place the crayons in the boxes in a specific pattern, such as ABAB.

- Option 3—Write a number on the front of each crayon box using a washable or dry-erase marker. Fill each box with the number of crayons written on the box.

CRAYON BOX

CRAYON BOX

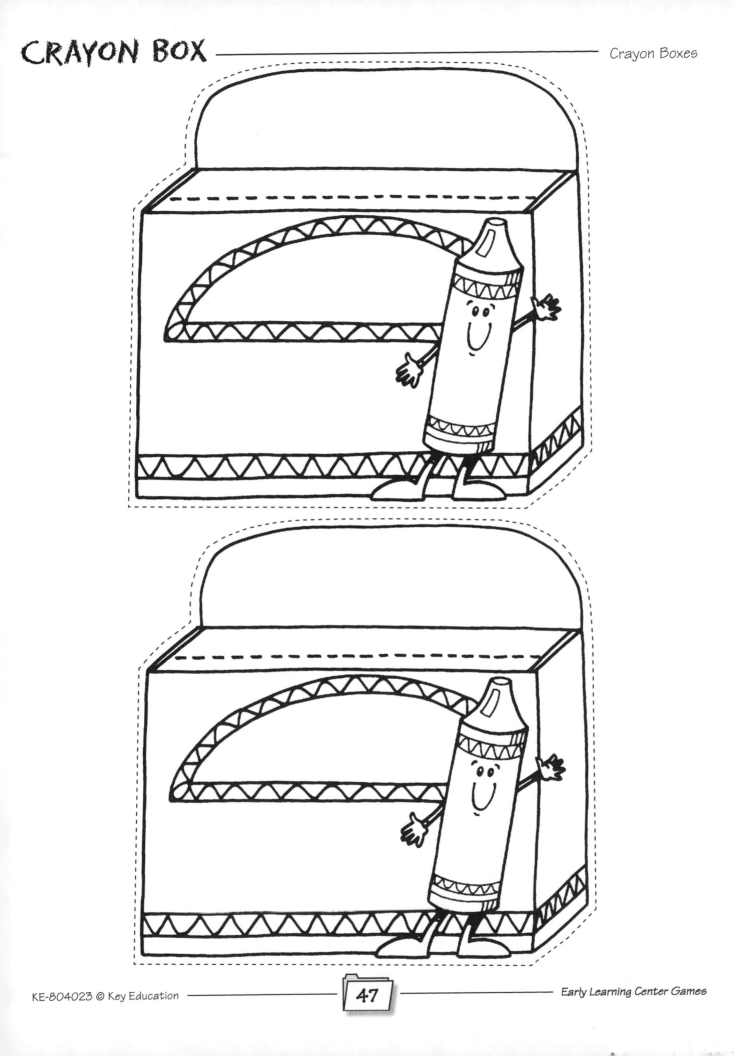

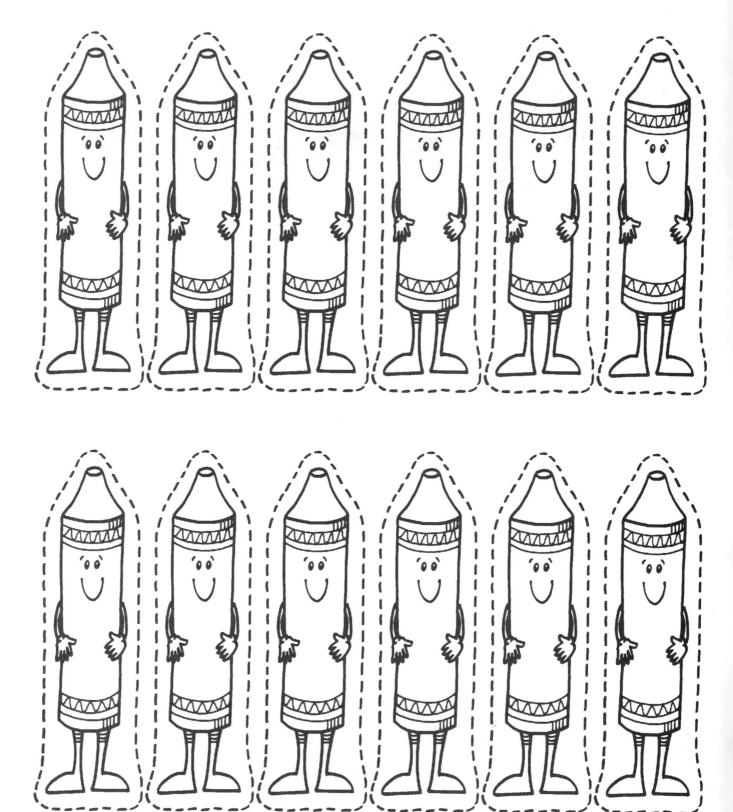

Make a Face

Themes: Body Parts, Emotions

Skill: Matching

Preparation:

1. Make two copies of the head line pattern (page 50). Cut out the figures along the frames.

2. Make one copy of the face card patterns (page 51). Color the cards as desired and cut apart along the dashed lines. Laminate each card separately and trim.

3. Make one copy of each facial features pattern (pages 52–54). Color as desired and cut out along the dashed lines. Laminate each piece separately and trim.

Assembly:

1. Glue the head lines to the inside of a file folder as shown above.

2. Attach the file folder name tag and the "To Play" instruction box on the outside of the file folder as shown on page 5.

3. Laminate the entire file folder. Trim around the edges.

4. Place all of the face cards in a plastic zippered sandwich bag. Place all of the facial feature pieces and a small ball of sticky-tack adhesive in a quart-sized zippered bag. Label each bag with a name tag and attach to the front of the file folder.

Extension:

Extend the activity by having the children create faces to show specific emotions. Example: "Can you make the face look angry?" Let the children use washable or dry-erase markers to add details as needed.

To Play:

- Shuffle the face cards and stack them in a pile, picture sides down. Draw one card from the top of the stack.

- Using the bag of facial features, create a face to match the one on the card by placing facial parts on the correct places.

Make a Face

Make a Face

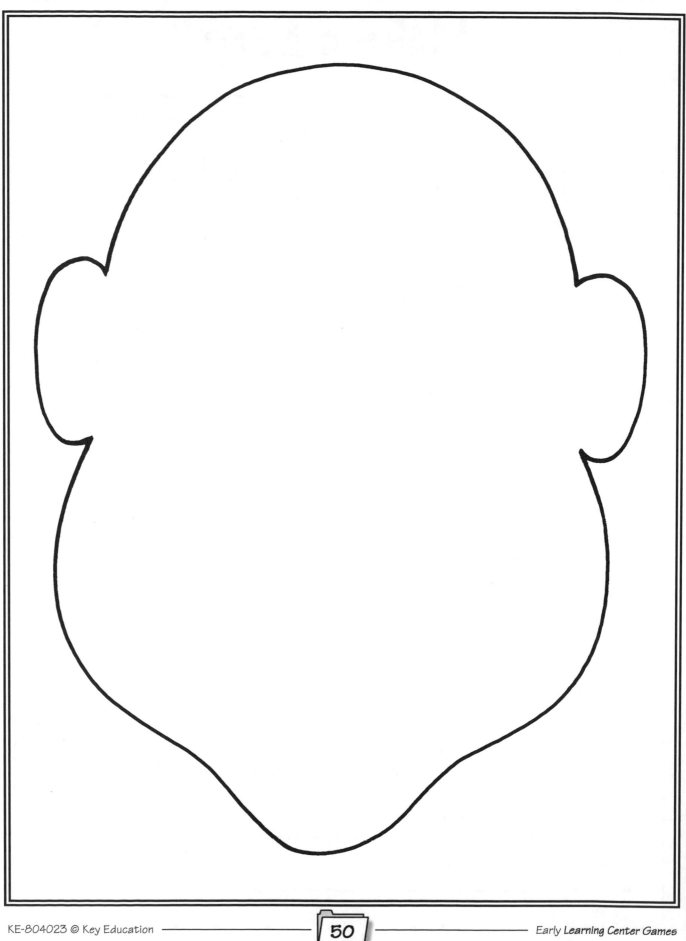

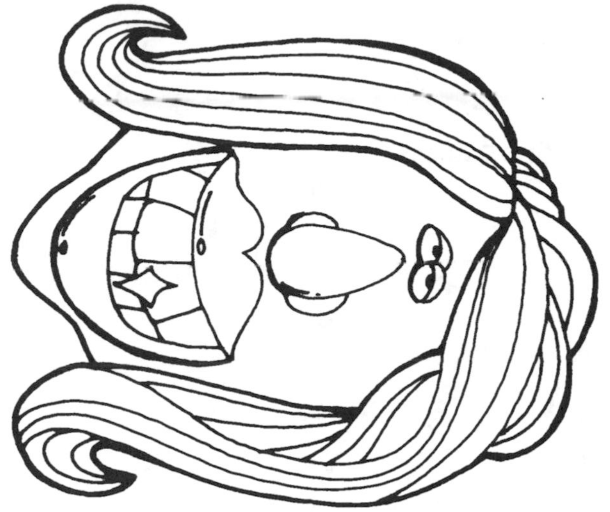
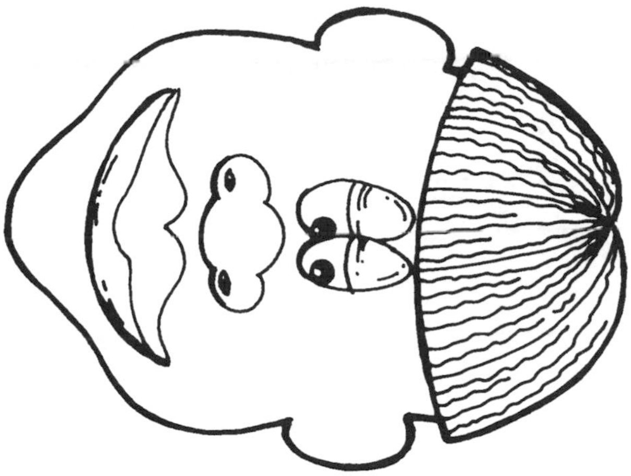
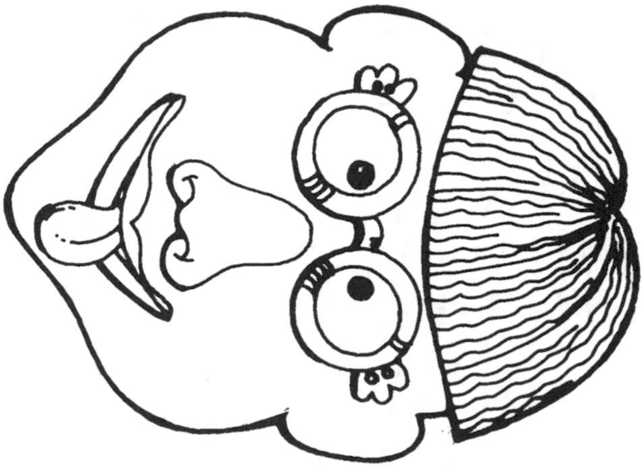
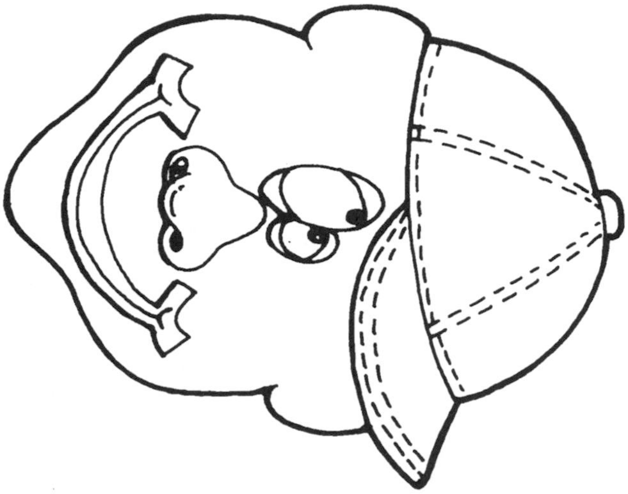
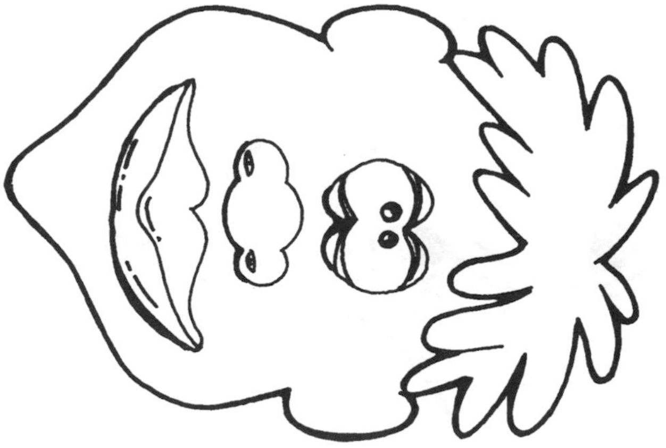
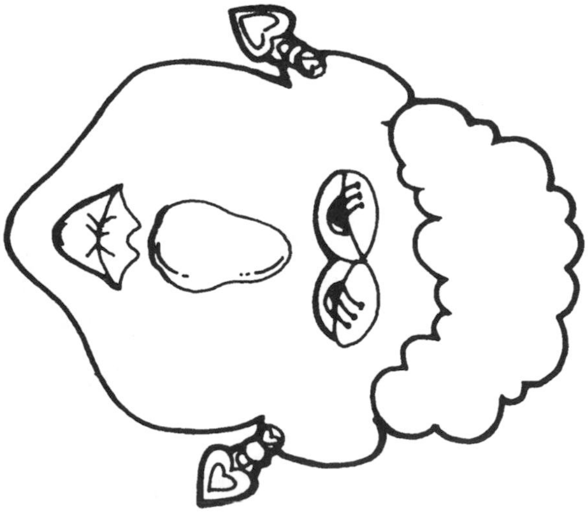

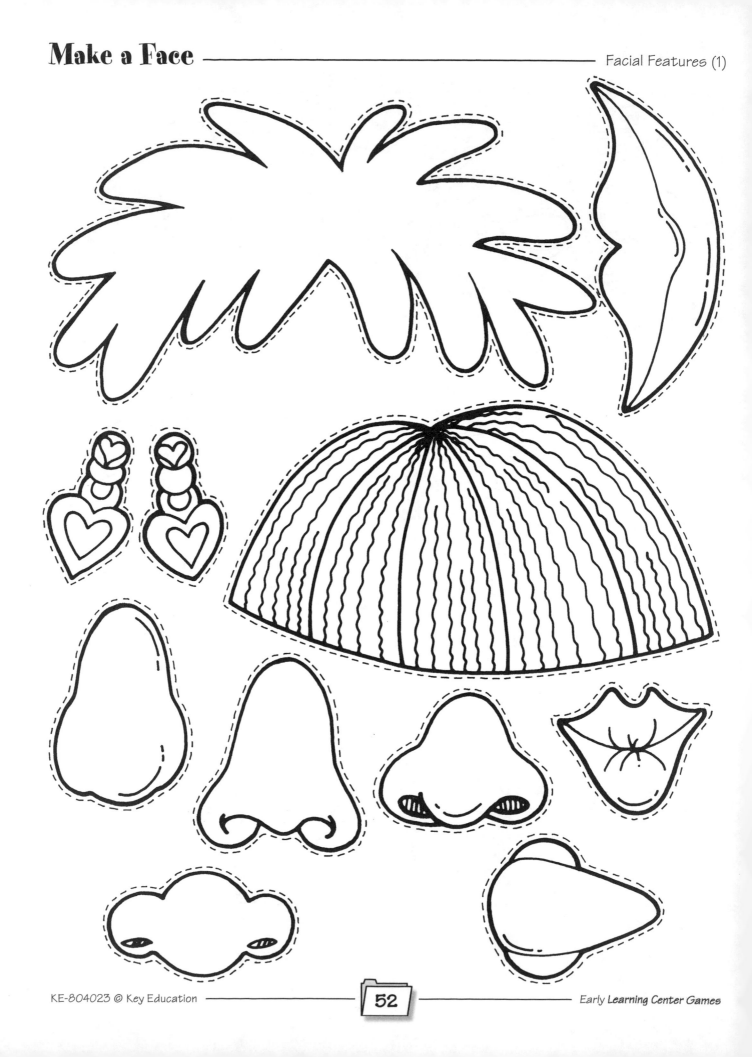

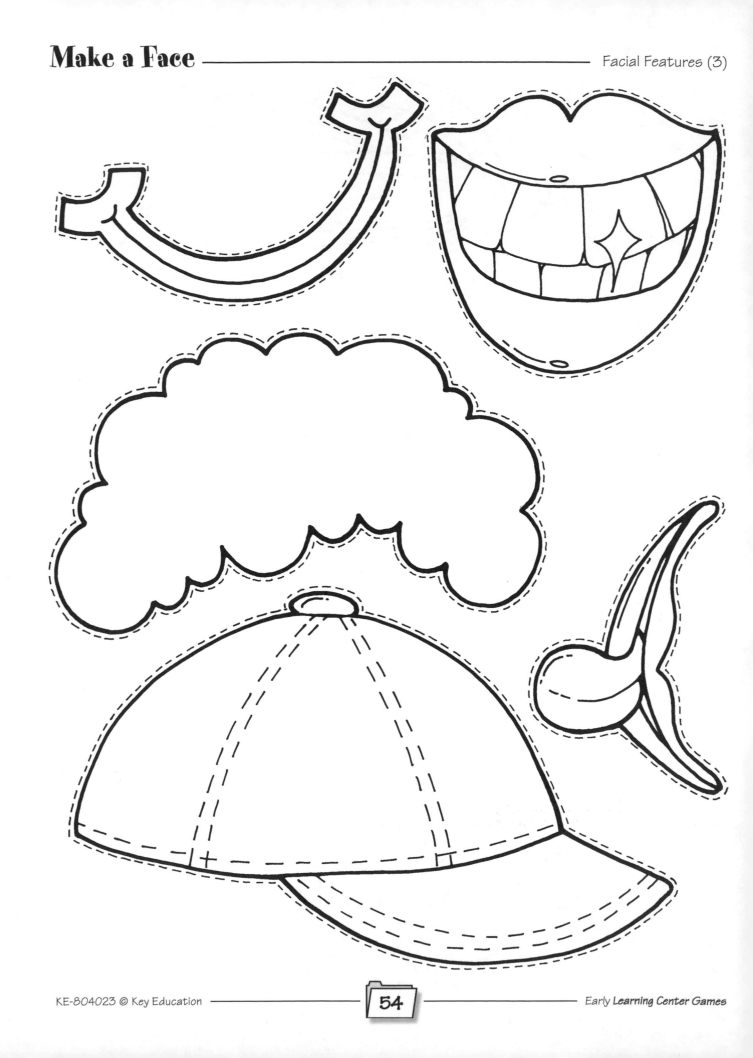

Community Helpers

Theme: Community Helpers

Skills: Matching, Knowledge of jobs and related activities

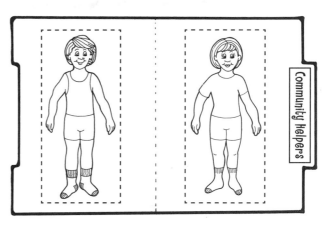

Preparation:

1. Make a copy of each of the community helper patterns (page 56). Color as desired and then cut out the figures along the dashed lines.

2. Make one copy of all the community helper uniforms, tools, and accessories patterns (pages 57–60). Color as desired and cut out along the dashed lines. Laminate each piece separately and trim.

Assembly:

1. Glue the two community helpers to the inside of a file folder as shown above.

2. Attach the file folder name tag and the "To Play" instruction box on the outside of the file folder as shown on page 5.

3. Laminate the entire file folder. Trim around the edges.

4. Place all of the uniforms, tools, and accessories along with a small ball of sticky-tack adhesive in a quart-sized plastic zippered bag. Label the bag with a name tag and attach to the front of the file folder.

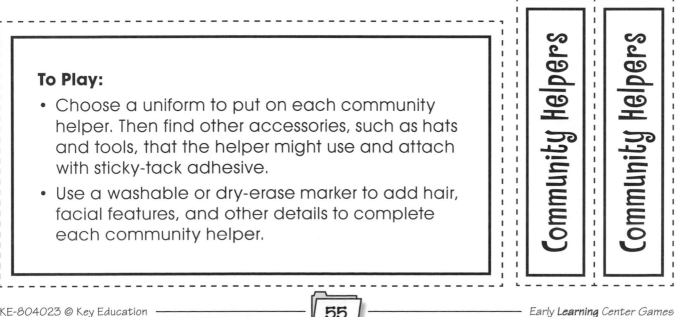

To Play:

- Choose a uniform to put on each community helper. Then find other accessories, such as hats and tools, that the helper might use and attach with sticky-tack adhesive.

- Use a washable or dry-erase marker to add hair, facial features, and other details to complete each community helper.

Community Helpers

Community Helpers

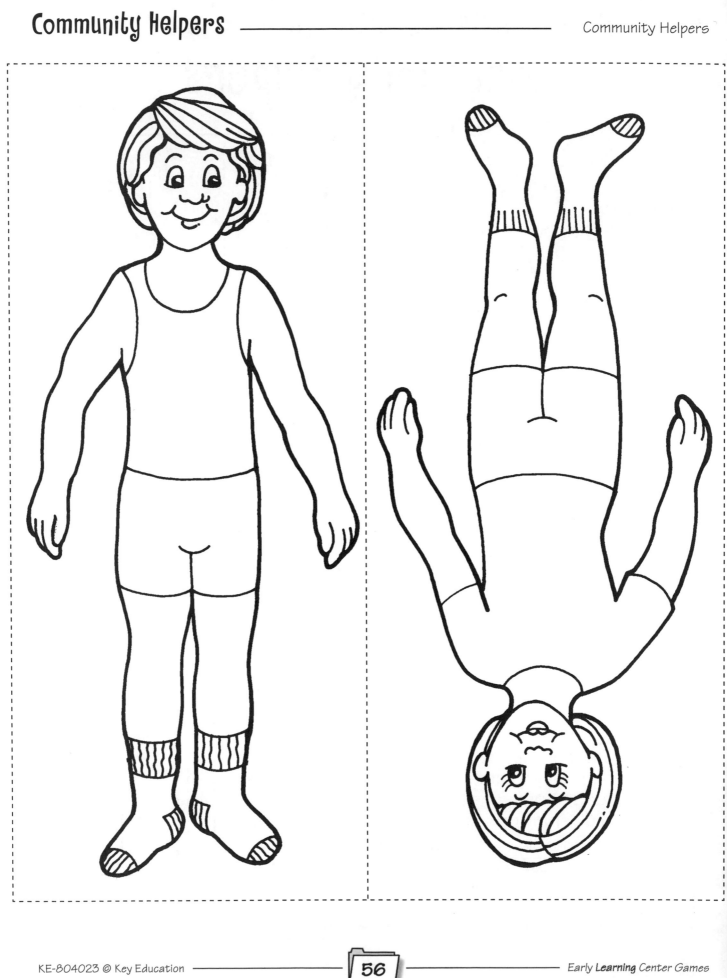

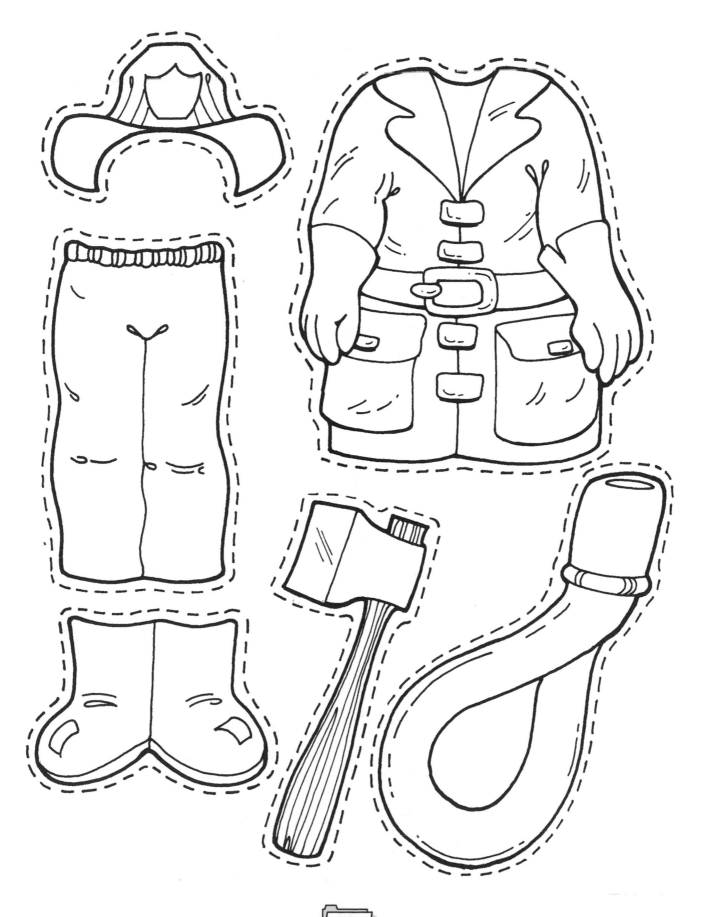

Community Helpers

58

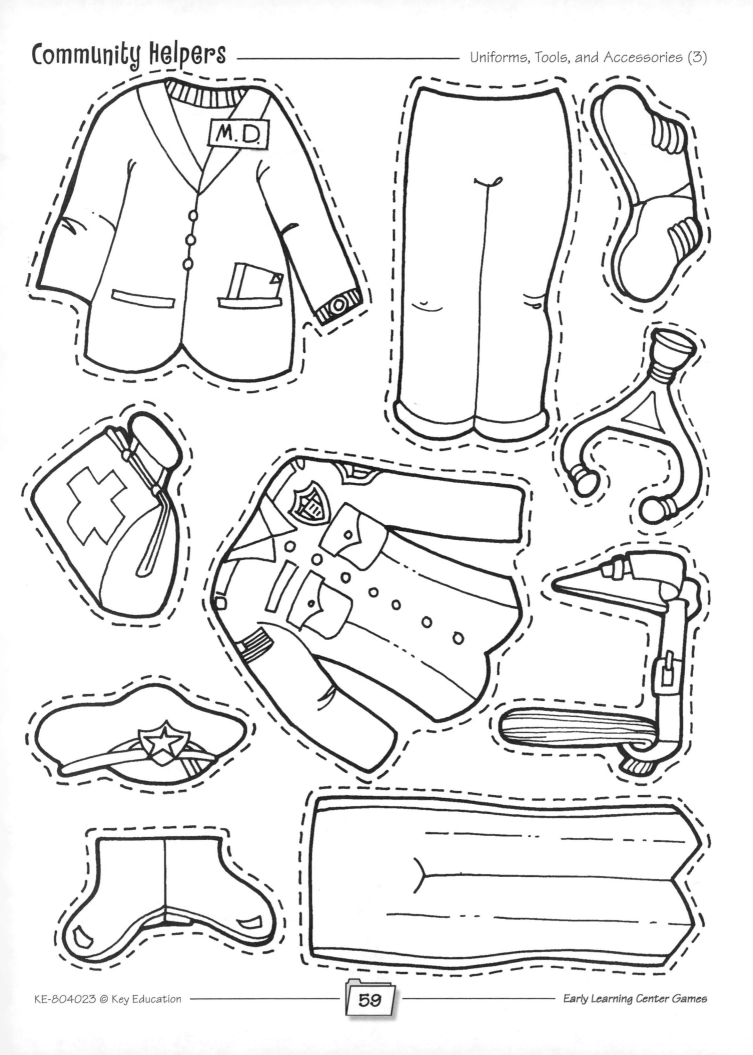

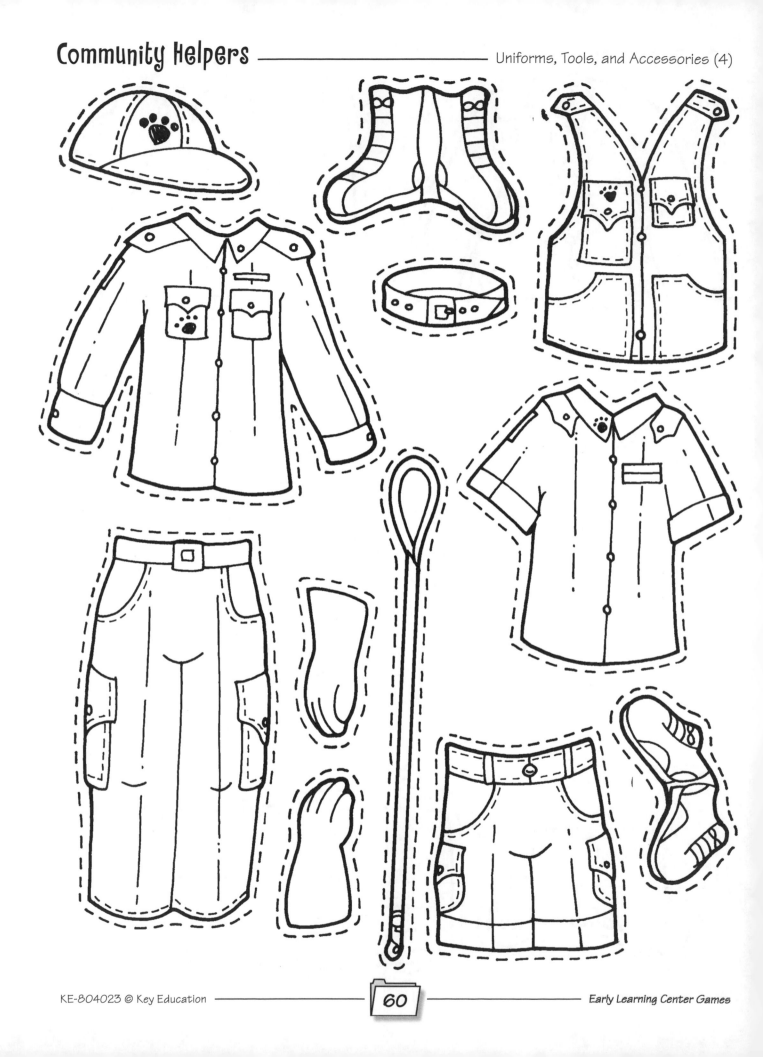

Family Portrait

Theme: Family

Skills: Counting, Sorting

Preparation:

1. Make two copies of the picture frame pattern (page 62). Color as desired. Cut out along the dashed line.

2. Make several copies of the family member patterns (pages 63–64). Color as desired. Cut out the figures along the dashed lines. Laminate each person separately and trim.

3. Make one copy of the family portrait cards (page 65). Cut apart the cards along the dashed lines. Laminate each card separately and trim.

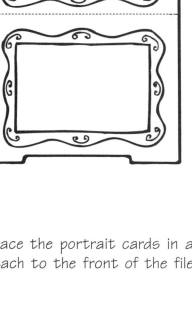

Assembly:

1. Glue the picture frames to the inside of a file folder as shown here.

2. Attach the file folder name tag and the "To Play" instruction box on the outside of the file folder as shown on page 5.

3. Laminate the entire file folder. Trim around the edges.

4. Place the family figures in a quart-sized plastic zippered bag. Place the portrait cards in a zippered sandwich bag. Label each bag with a name tag and attach to the front of the file folder.

Extension:

Extend the activity by having the children create their own family portraits. Provide several copies of the picture frames and family figures. After playing the file folder game, have the children create family portraits by gluing figures that correspond to their own family members inside the picture frames. Let the children color the figures as desired.

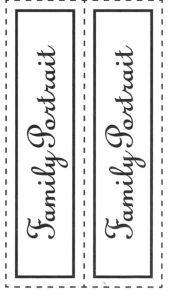

To Play:
- Draw a family portrait card from the bag.
- Add family members to one of the photo frames using the same number of adults/children and boys/girls as indicated on the card.
- Repeat to create a second family photograph.

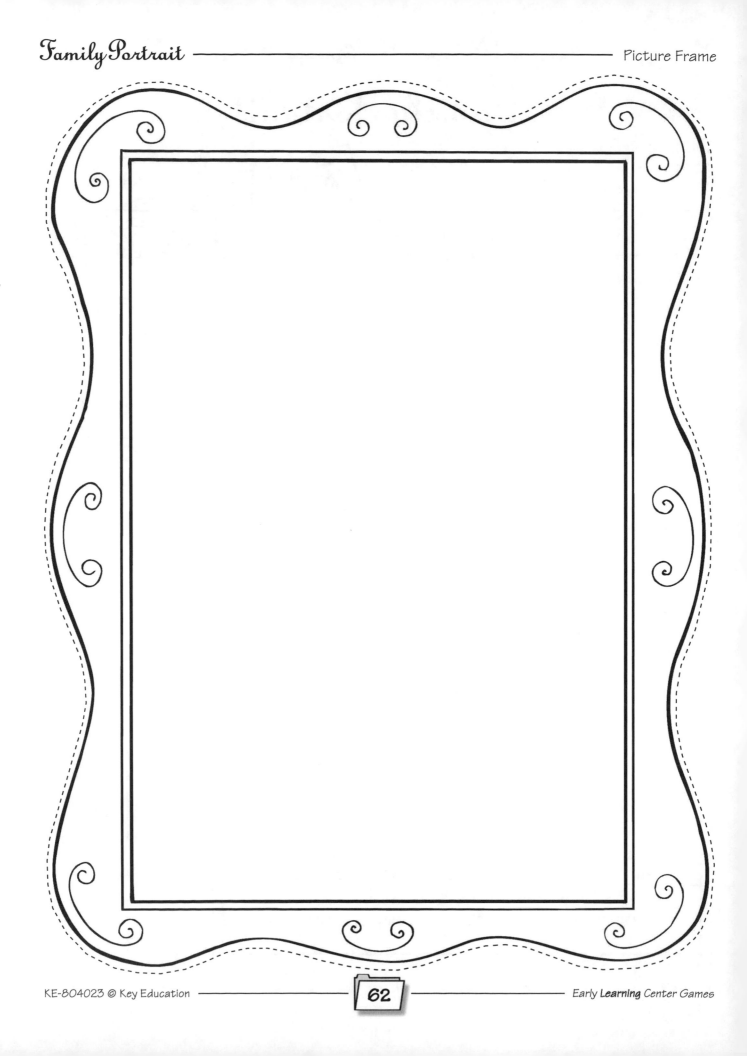

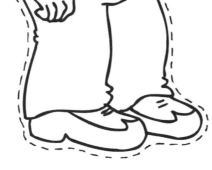

Safe / Not Safe

Theme: Safety
Skill: Categorizing

Preparation:

1. Make 10 copies of the smiling face and frowning-face bandage on this page. Cut out each figure. Laminate each figure separately and trim.

2. Make one copy of each safe/unsafe scenario patterns (pages 67–68). Color as desired. Trim each page along the solid lines.

Assembly:

1. Glue the two safe/unsafe scenario pages to the inside of a file folder as shown above.

2. Attach the file folder name tag and the "To Play" instruction box on the outside of the file folder as shown on page 5.

3. Laminate the entire file folder. Trim around the edges.

4. Place all of the smiling faces and frowning-face bandages along with a small ball of sticky-tack adhesive in a quart-sized plastic zippered bag. Label the bag with a name tag and attach to the front of the file folder.

To Play:

- Look at the picture in each box.
- If the picture shows a child being safe, stick a smiling face on the picture. If the picture shows a child being unsafe, stick a frowning-face bandage on the picture.

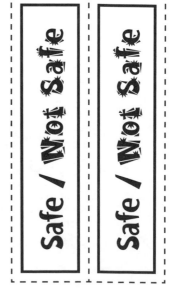

Playing with matches

Putting away toys

Running away from strangers

Standing on a slide

Give weapons to an adult

Wearing a bike helmet

Crossing the street with an adult

Standing on a toy

Standing on a swing

Wearing a seat belt

Chasing a ball into the street

Running with scissors

Healthy for Me

Themes: Health, Food

Skill: Categorizing

Preparation:

1. Make one copy each of the healthy and unhealthy food patterns (pages 70–71). Color the foods as desired and cut out each piece along the dashed lines. Laminate each piece separately and trim.

2. Make one copy each of the Healthy for Me and Unhealthy for Me patterns (pages 72–73). Color as desired and cut out along the solid black border. Laminate each page separately and trim.

Assembly:

1. Glue the Healthy for Me pattern to the left half of a file folder. Do not put glue in the space 1" (25 mm) below the dashed line drawn across the platter.

2. Glue the Unhealthy for Me pattern to the right half of the file folder. Do not put glue in the space 1" (25 mm) below the dashed line on the trash can.

3. Attach the file folder name tag and the "To Play" instruction box on the outside of the file folder as shown on page 5.

4. Laminate the entire file folder. Trim around the edges.

5. Use a craft knife to cut out pockets. Carefully cut through the laminated piece along the dashed lines on the serving platter and the trash can. Be sure not to cut through the file folder itself.

6. Place all of the food items in a quart-sized plastic zippered bag. Label the bag with a name tag and attach to the front of the file folder.

To Play:

- Look at the food items in the bag.
- Place the foods that are healthy for you in the pocket on the serving tray.
- Place the foods that are unhealthy for you in the pocket on the trash can.

Healthy for Me

Unhealthy for Me

Animal Babies

Theme: Animals

Skills: Letter recognition, Matching, Animals

Preparation:

1. Make one copy of the penguins below and each of the animal babies and parents patterns (pages 75–79). Color as desired and cut out each animal individually.

2. Set aside the adult animals (animals with uppercase letters on their bellies). Laminate each of the baby animals (animals with lowercase letters on their bellies) separately and trim.

Assembly:

1. Glue all of the adult animals to the inside of a file folder as shown above.

2. Attach the file folder name tag and the "To Play" instruction box on the outside of the file folder as shown on page 5.

3. Laminate the entire file folder. Trim around the edges.

4. Place all of the baby animals and a small ball of sticky-tack adhesive in a quart-sized plastic zippered bag. Label the bag with a name tag and attach to the front of the file folder.

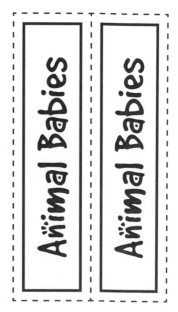

To Play:

- Help each animal find its baby.
- Match the lowercase and uppercase letters to put the baby animals with their parents.

Load the Train

Theme: Transportation

Skills: Beginning sounds, Letter recognition, Matching

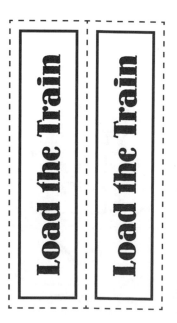

Preparation:

1. Make one copy of the train engine patterns (page 81). Color as desired and cut out along the dashed lines.

2. Make two copies of the train car patterns (page 82). Color as desired and cut out along the dashed lines. Laminate each train car separately and trim.

3. Make one copy each of the cargo patterns (pages 83–85). Color as desired and cut out along the dashed lines. Laminate each piece of cargo separately and trim.

Assembly:

1. Draw three simple train tracks across the inside of a file folder as shown above. Space the tracks evenly on the file folder as shown above.

2. Glue one train engine at the left end of each track. Glue the other three train engines just to the right of the center fold as shown.

3. Glue two matching train cars behind each corresponding engine. Glue only along the bottom and side edges, leaving the tops of the cars free of glue.

4. Attach the file folder name tag and the "To Play" instruction box on the outside of the file folder as shown on page 5.

5. Laminate the entire file folder. Trim around the edges.

6. Use a craft knife to cut out pockets. Carefully cut a slit through the laminate along the top edge only of each train car.

7. Place all of the cargo pieces in a quart-sized plastic zippered bag. Label the bag with a name tag and attach to the front of the file folder.

To Play:

- Look at the pieces of cargo.
- Slip each piece of cargo into a train car that is labeled with the same beginning sound.

Load the Train

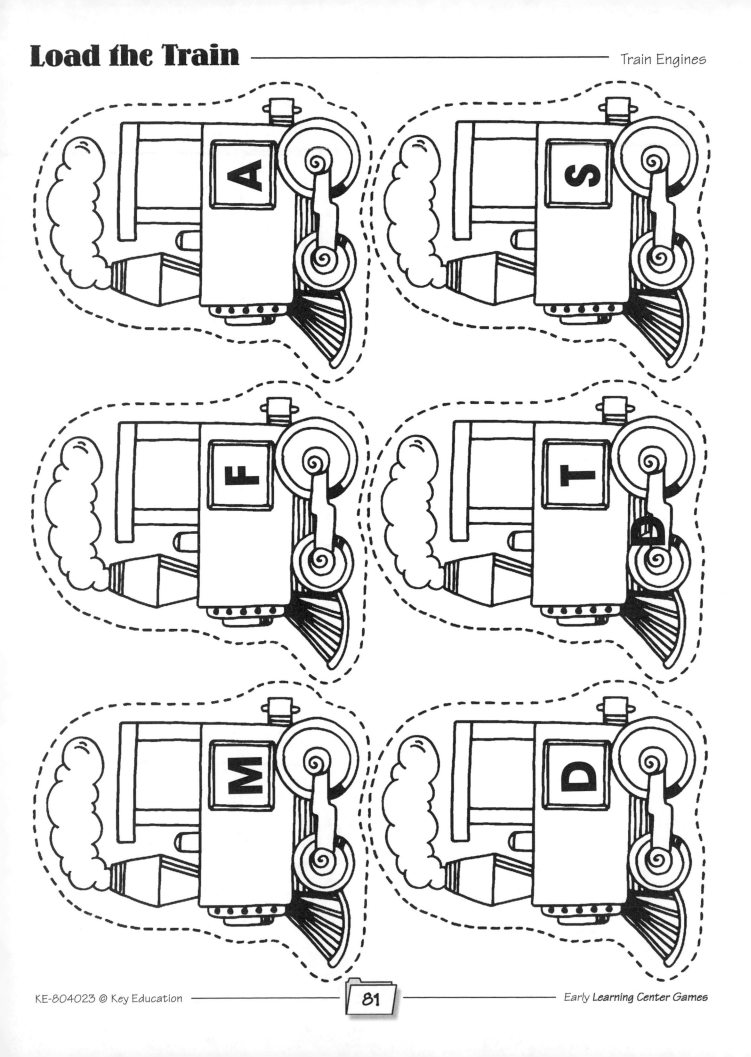

81

Load the Train

82

Load the Train

83

Load the Train

Load the Train

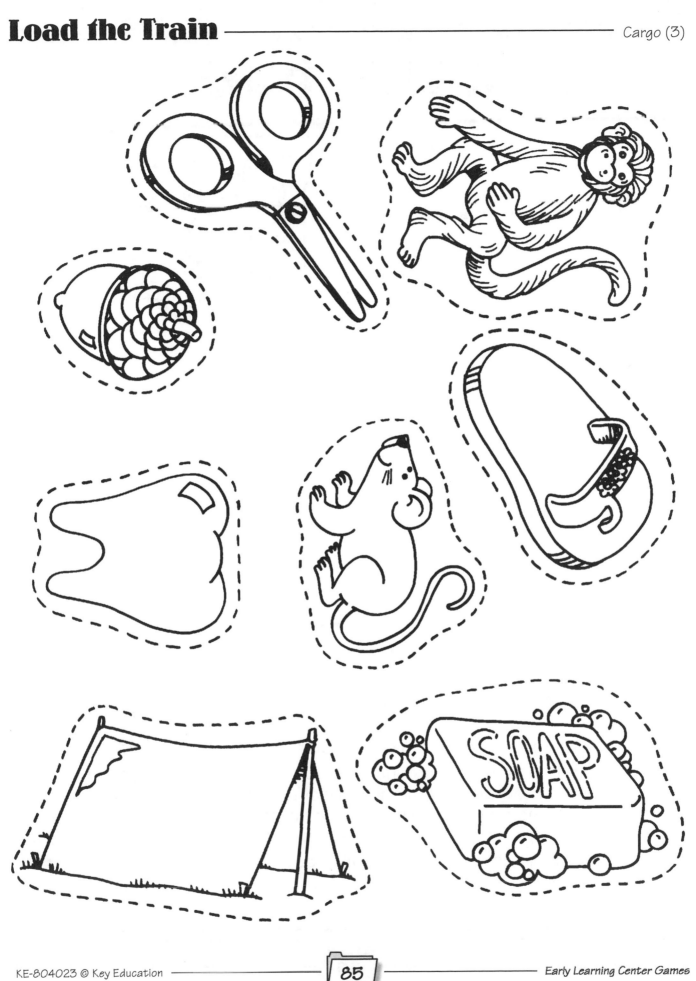

LEAPFROG

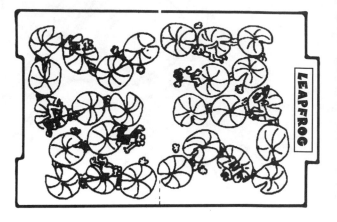

Theme: Animals

Skills: Number recognition, Counting

Preparation:

1. Make two copies of the lily pad game board (page 87). Color as desired and cut out.

2. Make 10 copies of the leapfrog game cards and bug patterns (page 88). Write a numeral or draw a set of dots on each leapfrog game card. Color as desired and cut apart the cards along the dashed lines. Laminate each card separately and trim.

Assembly:

1. Glue the lily pad game board to the inside of a file folder so that the borders meet at the center fold as shown above.

2. Attach the file folder name tag and the "To Play" instruction box on the outside of the file folder as shown on page 5.

3. Laminate the entire file folder. Trim around the edges.

4. Place the leapfrog cards and bugs in two separate plastic zippered sandwich bags. Label each bag with a name tag and attach to the front of the file folder.

To Play:

- Use a penny or an other small object as a game token to move around the lily pads.

- Place the cards face down on the table.

- Players take turns drawing one card from the deck and moving the same number of spaces as shown on the card. Each time a player passes a frog on a lily pad, that player collects one bug.

- After five minutes, players count their bugs and begin again.

Dinosaur Sort

Theme: Dinosaurs

Skills: Matching, Colors

Preparation:

1. Make four copies of the dinosaur patterns (page 90) on the following colors of paper: red, orange, yellow, green, blue, and purple. Cut out the dinosaurs along the dashed lines.

2. Set aside one dinosaur of each color. Laminate all of the other dinosaurs separately and trim.

Assembly:

1. Glue one dinosaur of each color to the inside of a file folder as shown above. Write the correct color word below each dinosaur.

2. Attach the file folder name tag and the "To Play" instruction box on the outside of the file folder as shown on page 5.

3. Laminate the entire file folder. Trim around the edges.

4. Gently poke a hole through the middle of each dinosaur on the file folder. Thread an 18" (46 cm) shoelace through each hole and knot around a matchstick on the back side of the file folder. Secure the matchsticks to the file folder with clear packing tape.

5. Punch a hole through the middle of each laminated cutout dinosaur.

6. Place all of the dinosaurs in a quart-sized plastic zippered bag. Label the bag with a name tag and attach to the front of the file folder.

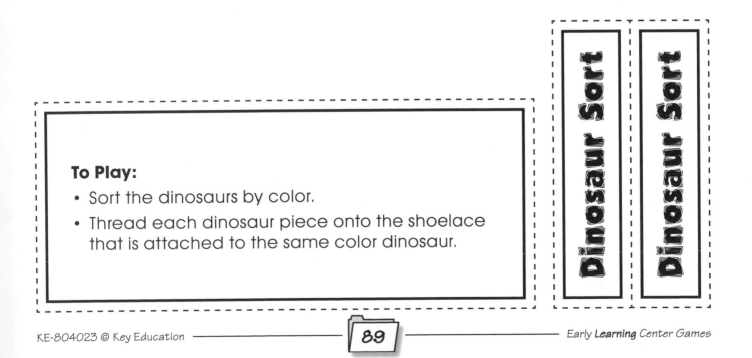

To Play:

- Sort the dinosaurs by color.
- Thread each dinosaur piece onto the shoelace that is attached to the same color dinosaur.

Dinosaur Sort

Dinosaur Sort

Dinosaur Sort

PLAY BALL!

Theme: Sports

Skills: Matching, Counting, Sets

Preparation:

1. Make three copies of the baseball player patterns (page 92). Discard two copies of the players or use them to decorate the outside of your file folder. Color as desired.

2. Make one copy of the baseball hat patterns (page 93). Color as desired.

3. Make one copy of the baseball patterns (page 94). Color as desired.

4. Cut out all of the players, hats, and balls along the dashed lines. Laminate each piece separately and trim.

Assembly:

1. Glue 10 baseball players to the inside of a file folder as shown above. Be sure to glue only around the outside edges of each player's glove. Leave at least 1" (25 mm) below the dashed line on the glove free of any glue.

2. Attach the file folder name tag and the "To Play" instruction box on the outside of the file folder as shown on page 5.

3. Laminate the entire file folder. Trim around the edges.

4. Use a craft knife to cut out pockets. Carefully cut a slit through the laminate and along the dashed line on each baseball glove . Be sure not to cut through the file folder itself.

5. Place the hats and the baseballs into two separate plastic zippered sandwich bags. Label each bag with a name tag and attach to the front of the file folder.

To Play:
- Place a hat on each baseball player.
- Slip the ball with the same number of dots into the pocket of the player's glove.

PLAY BALL!

PLAY BALL!

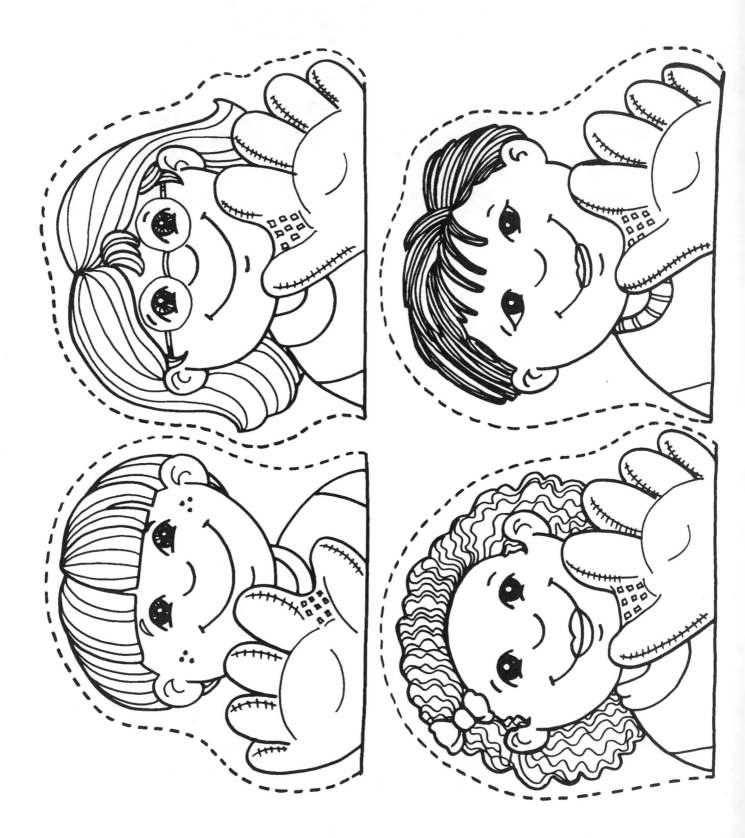

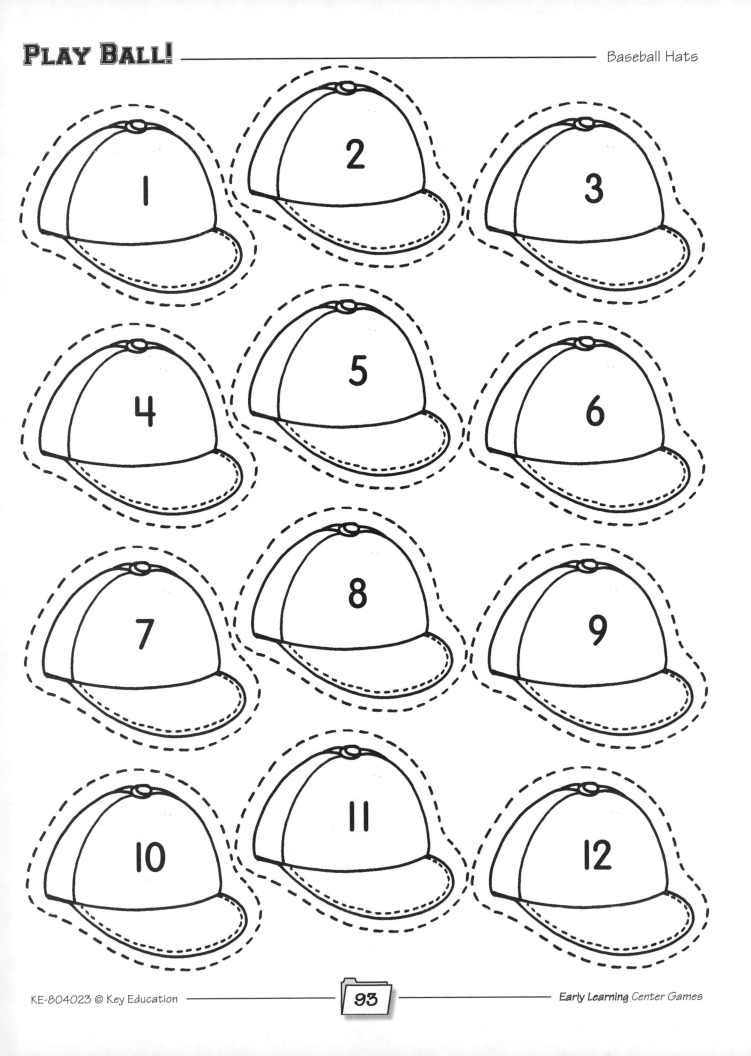

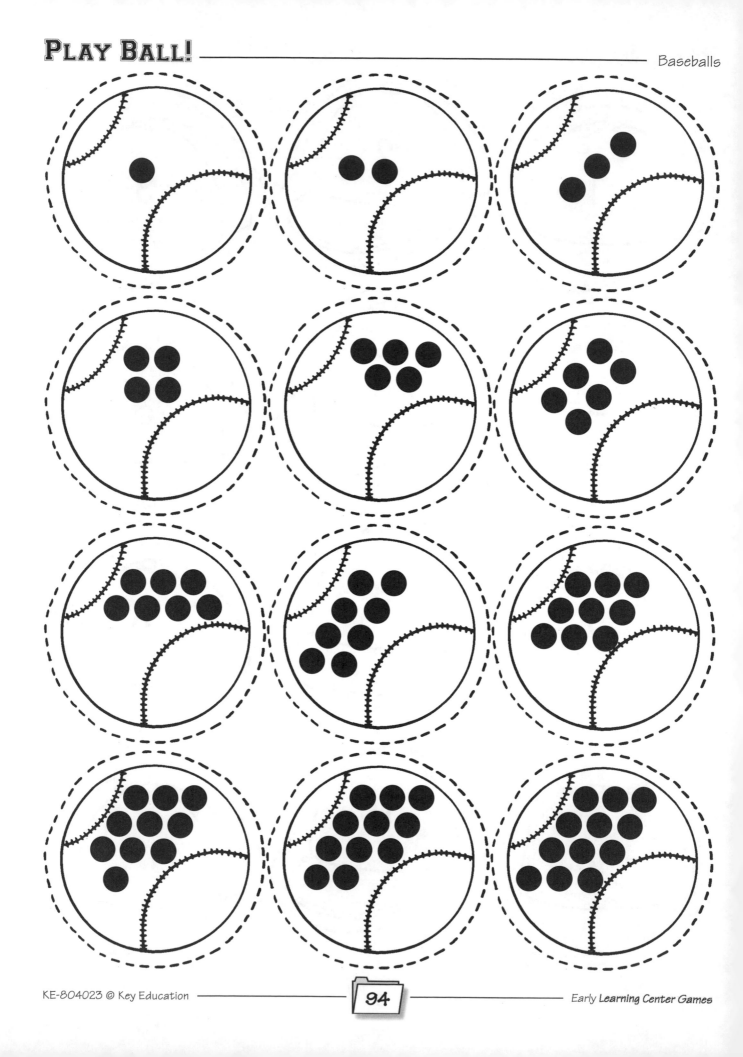

Swim Races

Themes: Summer, Sports

Skills: Counting, One-to-one correspondence

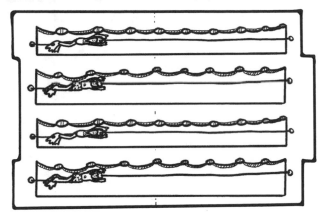

Preparation:

1. Make two copies of the swimmer and waves patterns (pages 96–97). Color as desired and cut out each figure along the dashed line.

2. Laminate each swimmer separately and trim.

3. Glue each set of three waves together by placing the left-hand side of one wave over the tab on the right-hand side of the previous wave. Cut off the tab on the end of the third wave.

Assembly:

1. Glue the waves to the inside of a file folder as shown above.

2. Attach the file folder name tag and the "To Play" instruction box on the outside of the file folder as shown on page 5.

3. Laminate the entire file folder. Trim along the edges.

4. Punch a hole through the file folder at the left and right ends of each wave as shown. Punch small holes in each swimmer where indicated by small dots on the feet and head.

5. Tie a 36" (90 cm) length of durable string to the head of one swimmer. Lay the swimmer on top of a wave and pull the string through the hole punched at the right end of the wave. Wrap the string across the back of the file folder and pull it through the hole at the left end of the wave. Adjust the string so there is very little slack and tie the other end to the swimmer's foot. Cut off any excess string.

6. Repeat step 5 with the remaining swimmers.

7. Place a die in a snack-sized plastic zippered bag. Label the bag with a name tag and attach to the front of the file folder.

To Play:

- Begin with all four swimmers at the left-hand side of the folder. Take turns rolling the die.

- Gently tug on the string to move the swimmer the same number of buoys as indicated by the number on the die. The first swimmer to reach the other side wins the race.

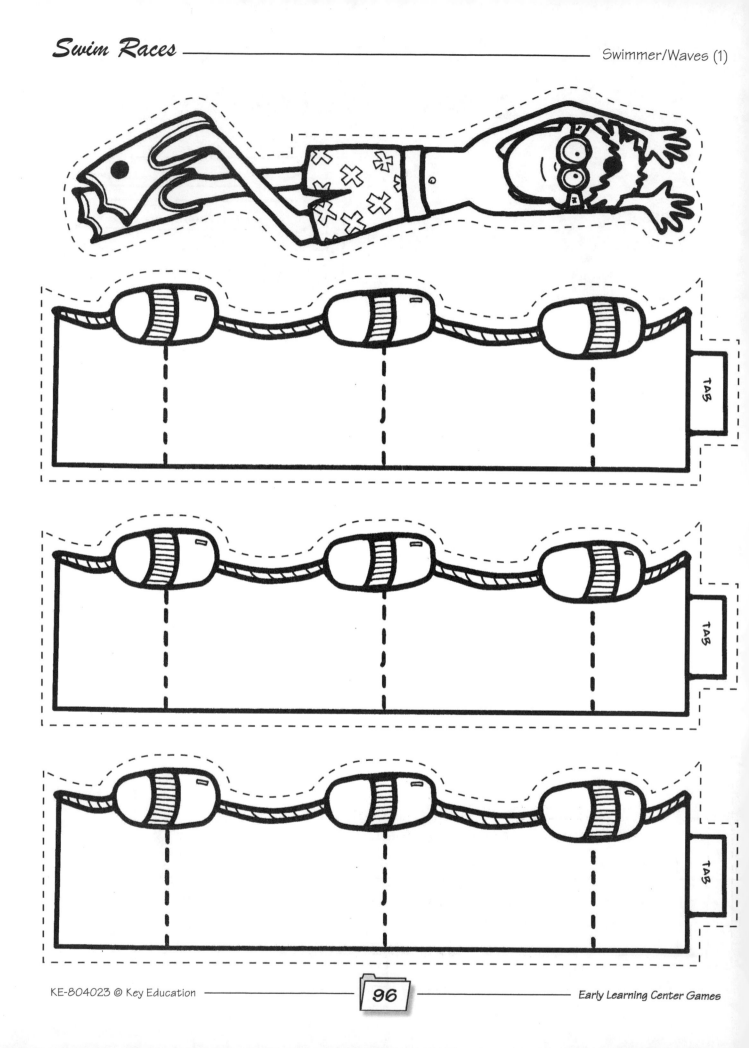

TAB

TAB

TAB

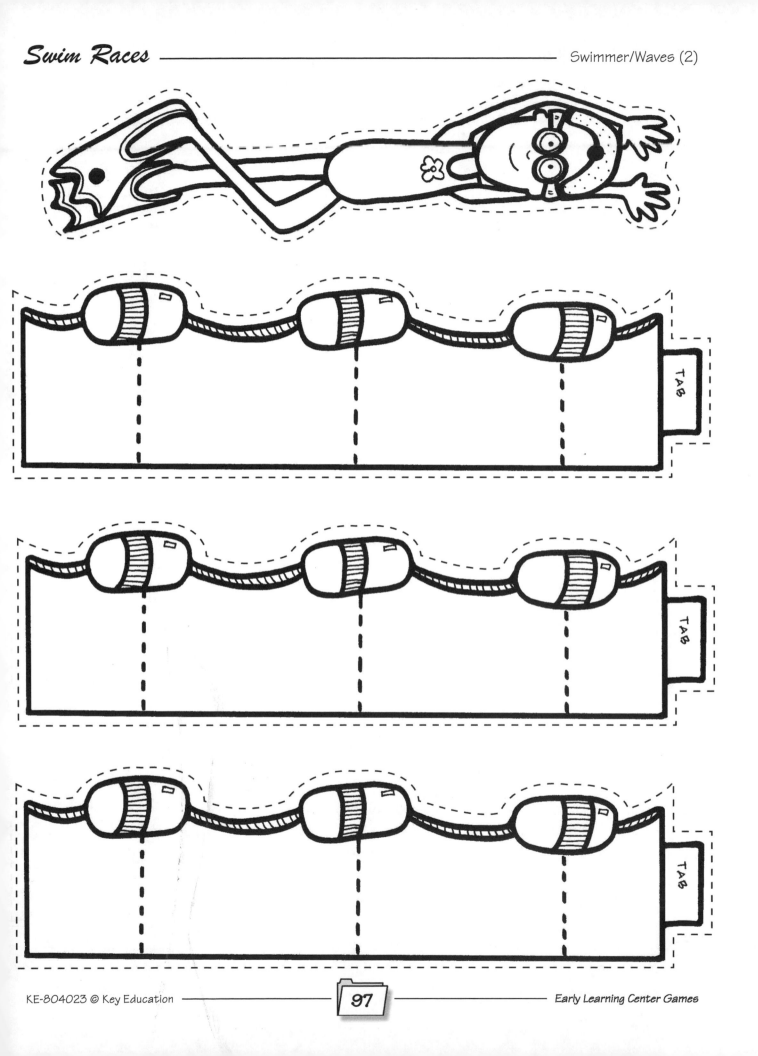

TAB

TAB

TAB

X-RAY ABC'S

Theme: Alphabet

Skills: Writing, Letter recognition

Preparation:

1. Make one copy of the X-ray machine pattern (page 99). Color as desired. Cut out along the solid black line and cut out the inside of the machine where indicated. Laminate and trim around the outside edges.

2. Make 26 copies of the skeleton pattern (page 100) on an assortment of colorful paper. Cut out the skeletons along the dashed lines.

3. Make one copy of each alphabet card patterns (pages 101–103) on white paper. Cut apart the cards along the dashed lines.

4. Glue one alphabet card inside the framed box on each skeleton. Laminate the skeletons and trim.

Assembly:

1. Glue a white sheet of paper to the inside of a file folder. Glue or tape the laminated x-ray machine over the piece of white paper along the side edges only. Leave the top and bottom edges free.

2. Attach the file folder name tag and the "To Play" instruction box on the outside of the file folder as shown on page 5.

3. Laminate the entire file folder. Trim around the edges.

4. Use a craft knife to cut out a window in the X-ray machine. Carefully cut through the laminate across the top and bottom edges only of the machine. Be sure not to cut through the file folder itself.

5. Place the alphabet skeletons in a gallon-sized plastic zippered bag. Label the bag with a name tag and attach to the front of the file folder.

To Play:
- Slide each skeleton into the x-ray machine so that the letters show through the window.
- Using a washable or dry-erase marker, trace the letters you see.
- Remove the skeleton, erase the letters, and x-ray a new body.

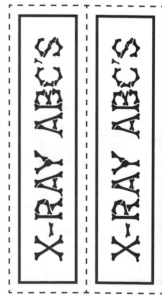

cut out

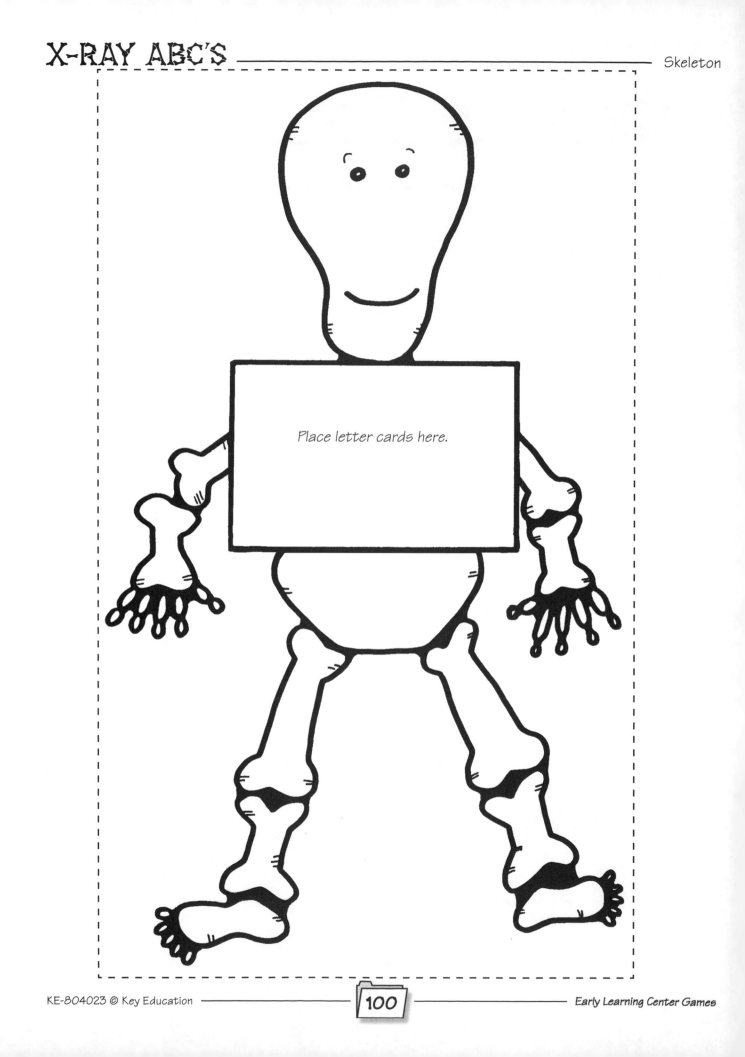

Place letter cards here.

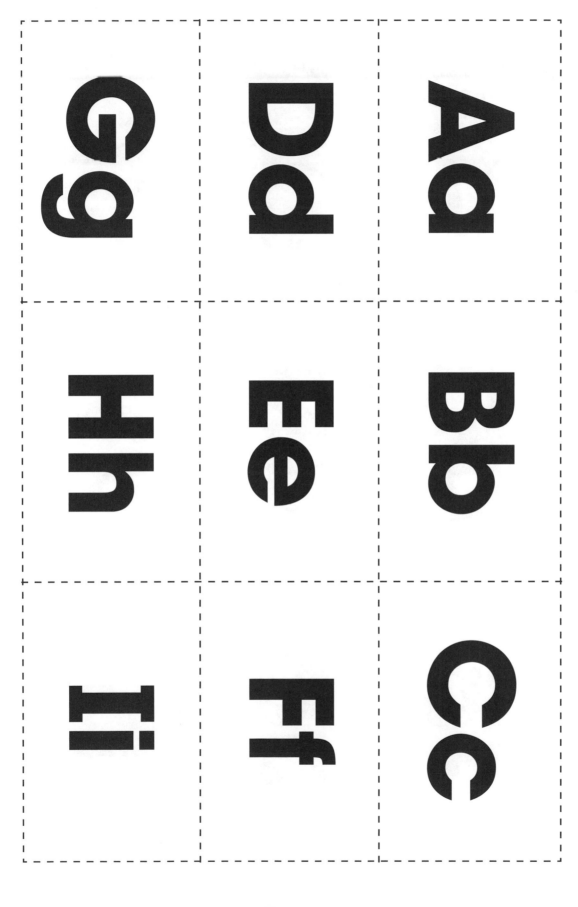

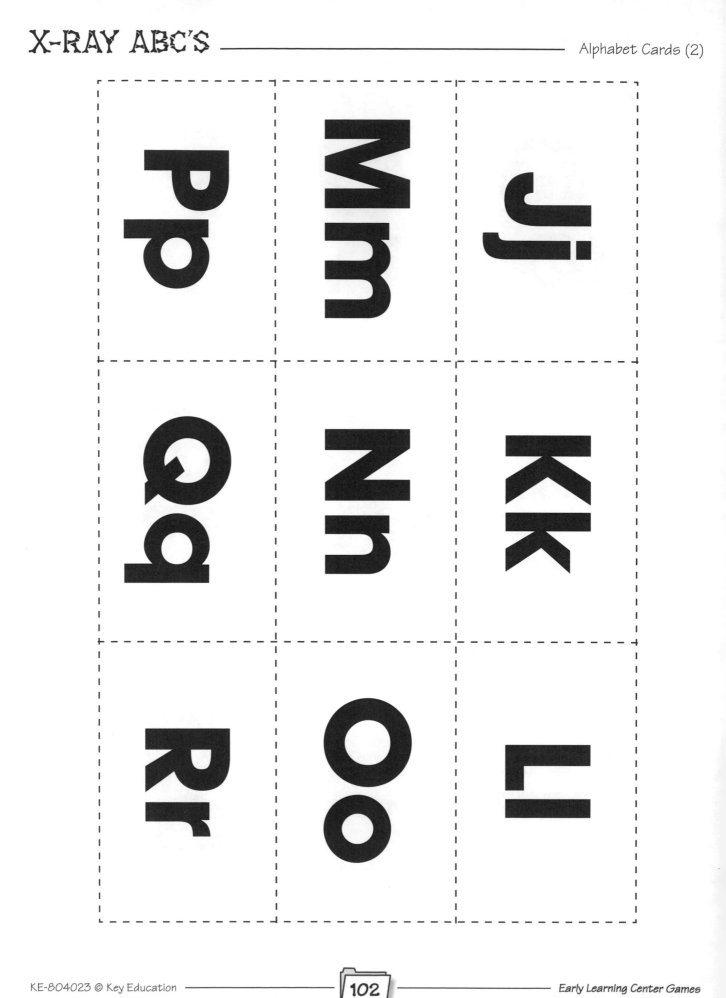

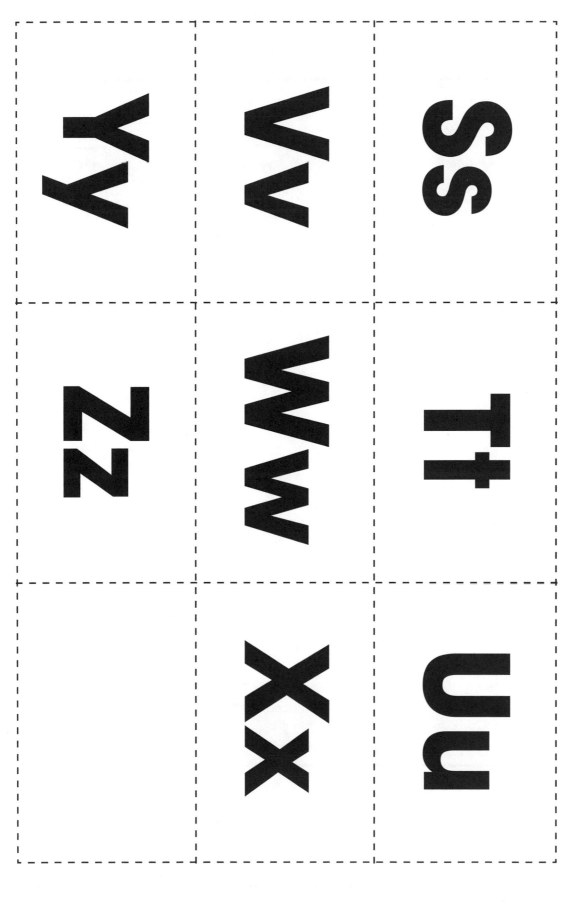

Special Delivery

Theme: Community Helpers

Skills: Matching, Colors, Number recognition, Number operations, Letter recognition

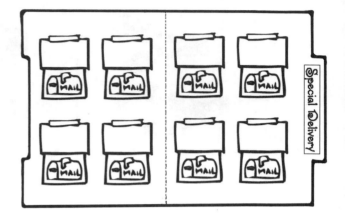

Preparation:

1. Make eight copies of the mailbox and envelope patterns (pages 105–106) on an assortment of colorful papers.

   - If making a color-matching game, write the name of each color on the front of the envelopes. Have the children match each envelope to the same color mailbox.

   - If making a number or math game, draw dots or write simple math sentences on the envelopes and corresponding numbers or answers on the mailboxes.

   - If making a letter-matching game, write lowercase letters on the envelopes and uppercase letters on the mailboxes.

2. Cut out all of the mailboxes and envelopes. Laminate each piece separately and trim.

Assembly:

1. Glue the eight mailboxes to the inside of a file folder as shown above. Glue only along the bottom and side edges of each mailbox, leaving the top free.

2. Attach the file folder name tag and the "To Play" instruction box on the outside of the file folder as shown on page 5.

3. Laminate the entire file folder. Trim around the edges.

4. Using a craft knife, carefully cut a slit through the laminate along the top edge of each mailbox to create a pocket. Be sure not to cut through the file folder itself.

5. Tape or glue each mailbox cover (apply glue only above the dashed line) so that it overlaps the top of the mailbox.

6. Place all of the envelopes in a quart-sized plastic zippered bag. Label the bag with a name tag and attach to the front of the file folder.

To Play:
- Lift the flaps to deliver the envelopes.
- Put each envelope in the matching mailbox.

Special Delivery

Special Delivery

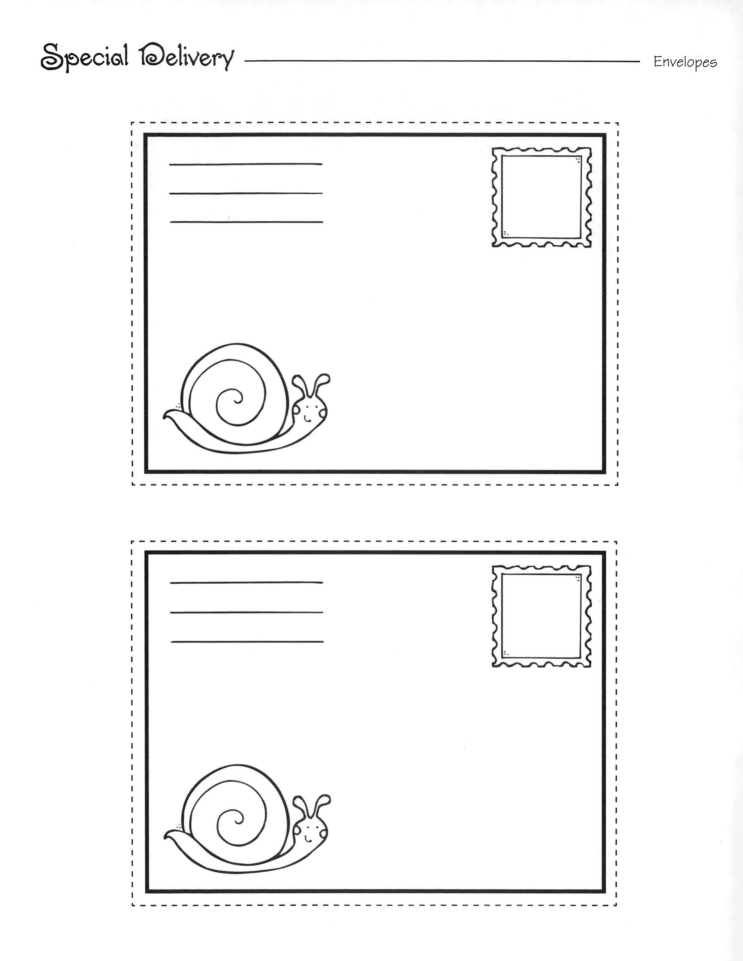

DAY AND NIGHT

Theme: Day and Night

Skills: Sorting, Time

Preparation:

1. Make one copy of both the daytime and nighttime frame patterns (pages 108–109). Color as desired and trim along the dashed lines.

2. Make one copy of all of the daytime/nighttime objects and activities patterns (pages 110–112). Color as desired and cut apart the cards along the dashed lines. Laminate each card separately and trim.

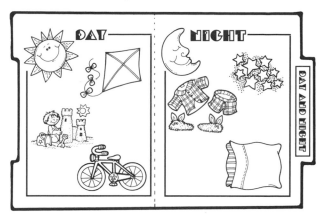

Assembly:

1. Glue the daytime frame onto the left half of a file folder as shown above. Glue the nighttime frame onto the right half of the file folder.

2. Attach the file folder name tag and the "To Play" instruction box on the outside of the file folder as shown on page 5.

3. Laminate the entire file folder. Trim around the edges.

4. Place all of the daytime/nighttime objects and activity cards, along with a small ball of sticky-tack adhesive, in a quart-sized plastic zippered bag. Label the bag with a name tag and attach to the front of the file folder.

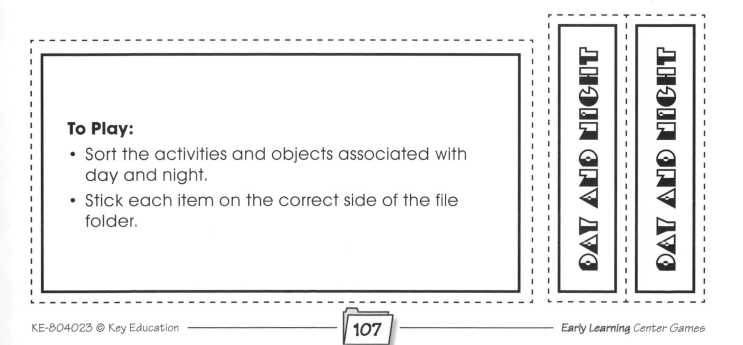

To Play:

- Sort the activities and objects associated with day and night.

- Stick each item on the correct side of the file folder.

DAY

NIGHT

HOT or Cold

Theme: Seasons

Skills: Sorting, Temperature

Preparation:

1. Make one copy of both the hot and cold banner/objects patterns (pages 114–115).

2. Color as desired and cut out the images along the dashed lines.

3. Set aside the hot and cold banners. Laminate all of the other pieces separately and trim.

Assembly:

1. Glue a sheet of red paper to the left half of a file folder. Glue a sheet of blue paper to the right half of the file folder.

2. Glue the "hot" banner at the top of the red sheet of paper. Glue the "cold" banner at the top of the blue sheet of paper.

3. Attach the file folder name tag and the "To Play" instruction box on the outside of the file folder as shown on page 5.

4. Laminate the entire file folder. Trim around the edges.

5. Place all of the hot and cold objects, along with a small ball of sticky-tack adhesive, in a quart-sized plastic zippered bag. Label the bag with a name tag and attach to the front of the file folder.

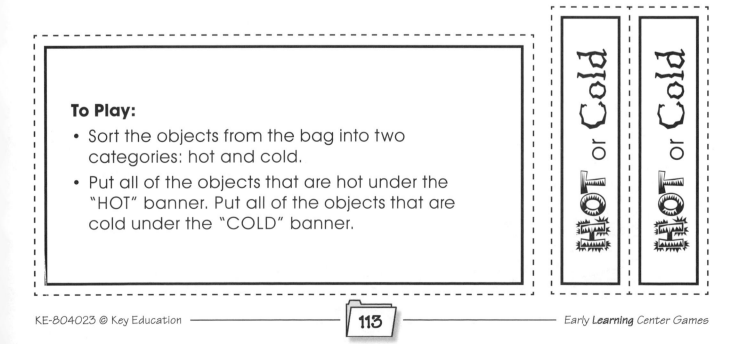

To Play:

- Sort the objects from the bag into two categories: hot and cold.

- Put all of the objects that are hot under the "HOT" banner. Put all of the objects that are cold under the "COLD" banner.

Dressed for the Season

Themes: Seasons, Clothing

Skill: Knowledge of seasons and related activities

Preparation:

1. Make one copy of all of the season patterns (pages 117–118). Color as desired. Cut out along the dashed lines.

2. Make one copy of all the seasonal clothing/accessories patterns (pages 119–121). Color as desired. Cut out along the dashed lines. Laminate each piece separately and trim.

Assembly:

1. Glue the four seasonal patterns to the inside of a file folder as shown.

2. Attach the file folder name tag and the "To Play" instruction box on the outside of the file folder as shown on page 5.

3. Laminate the entire file folder. Trim around the edges.

4. Place all of the seasonal clothing pieces and a small ball of sticky-tack adhesive in a quart-sized plastic zippered bag. Label the bag with a name tag and attach to the front of the file folder.

To Play:

- Dress the children appropriately for each season of the year.

- Take the clothing and accessories and stick them on the children to help them dress for the weather.

Dressed for the Season

Dressed for the Season

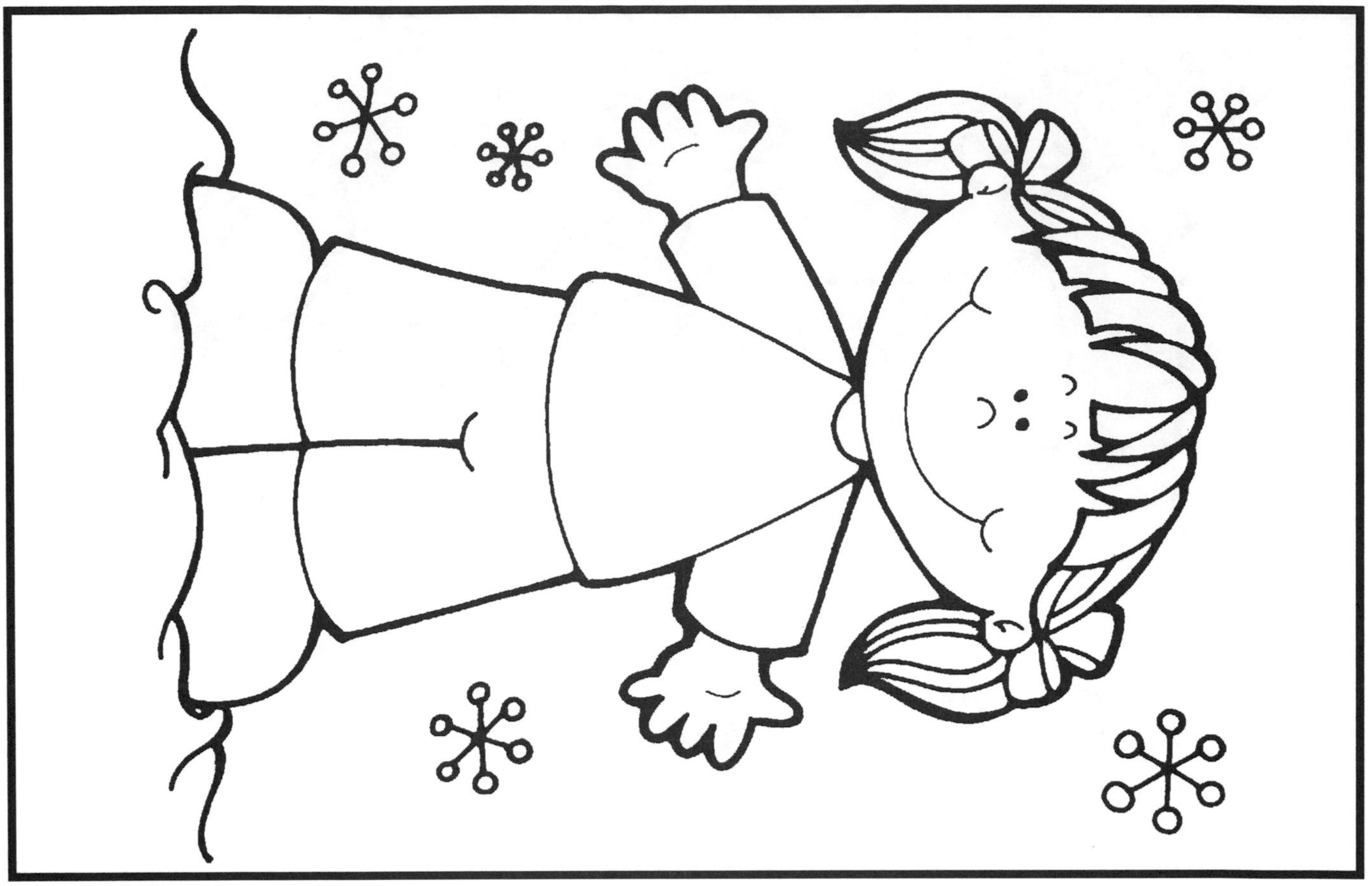

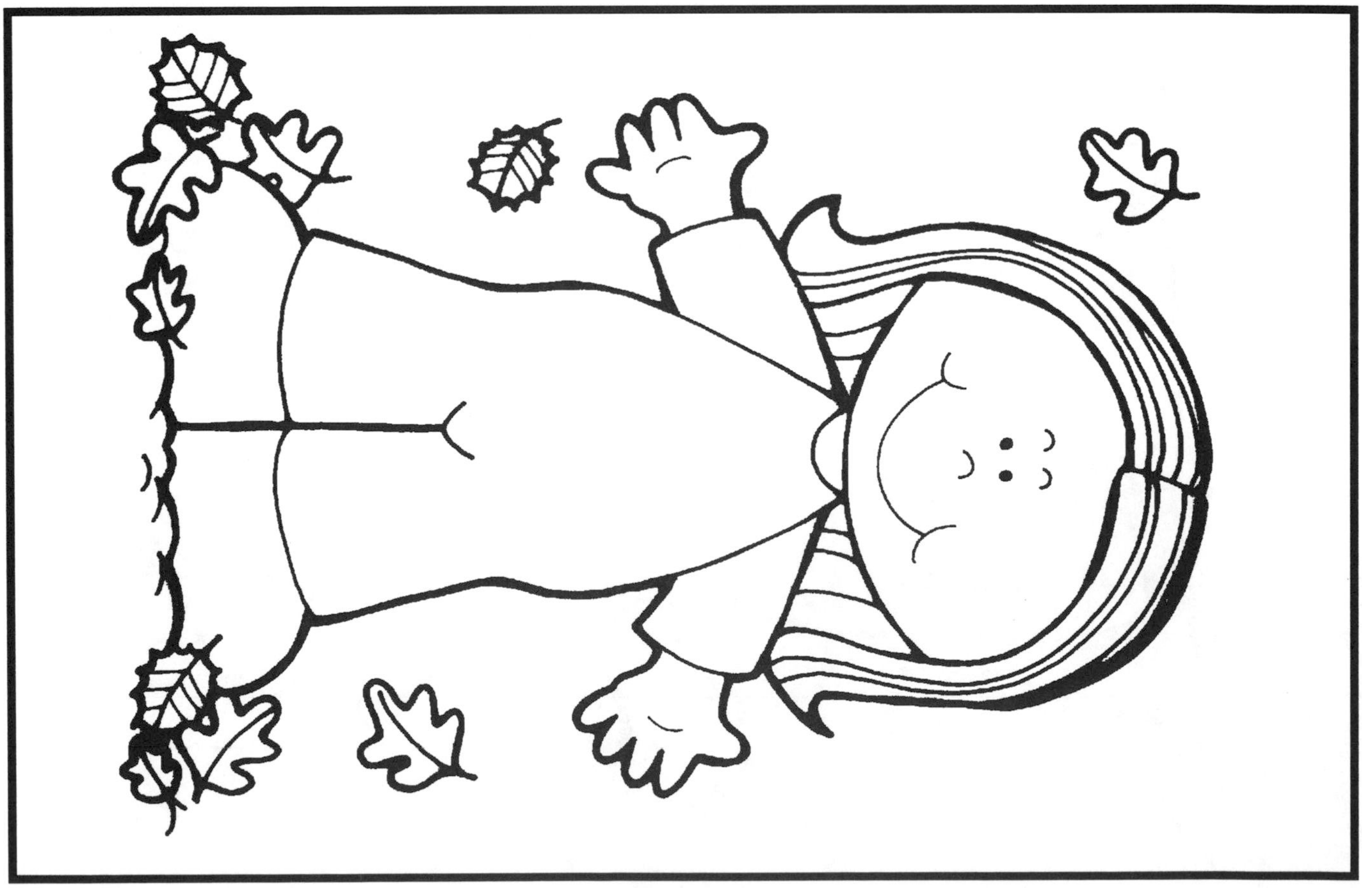

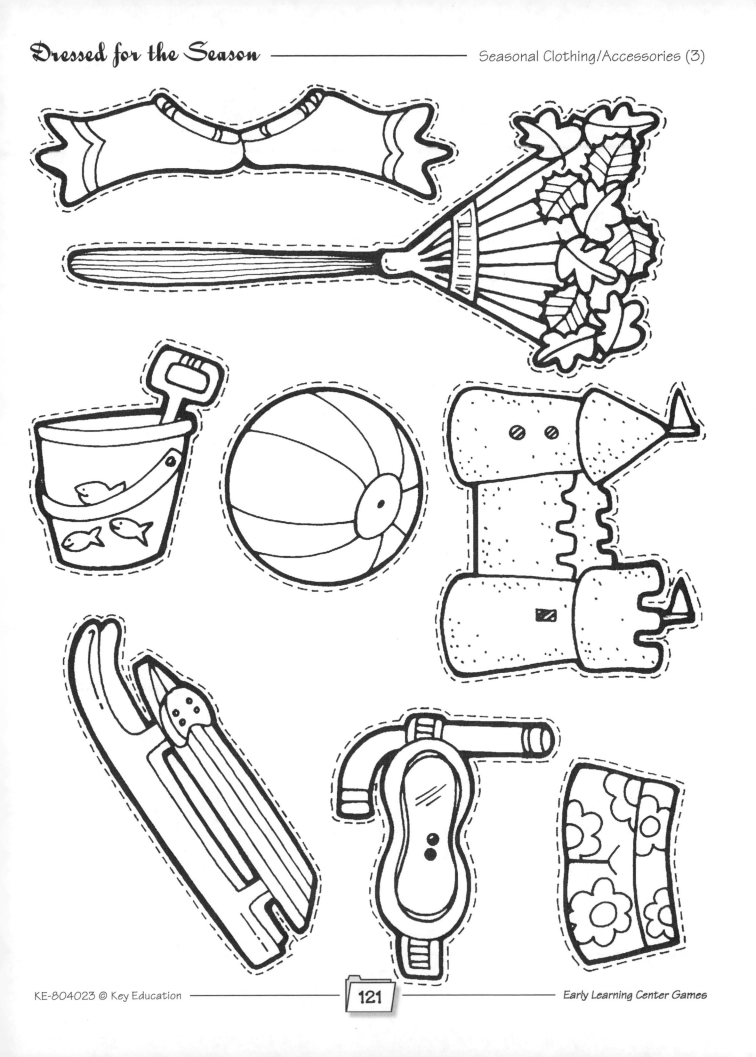

SNOWPERSON

Theme: Winter

Skills: Counting, Number recognition

Preparation:

1. Make four copies of the snowpeople patterns (page 123).
2. Color as desired and cut out each snowperson separately.

Assembly:

1. Glue the eight snowpeople to the inside of a file folder as shown above. Write a different number (e.g., 1–8) on each snowperson's hat.
2. Attach the file folder name tag and the "To Play" instruction box on the outside of the file folder as shown on page 5.
3. Laminate the entire file folder. Trim around the edges.
4. Place an assortment of colored buttons and a small ball of sticky-tack adhesive in a quart-sized plastic zippered bag. Label the bag with a name tag and attach to the front of the file folder.

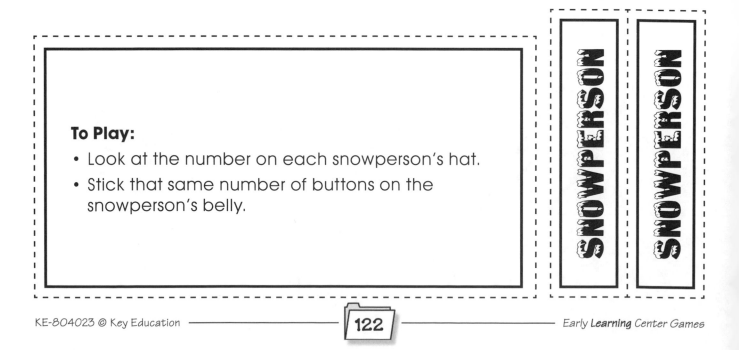

To Play:

- Look at the number on each snowperson's hat.
- Stick that same number of buttons on the snowperson's belly.

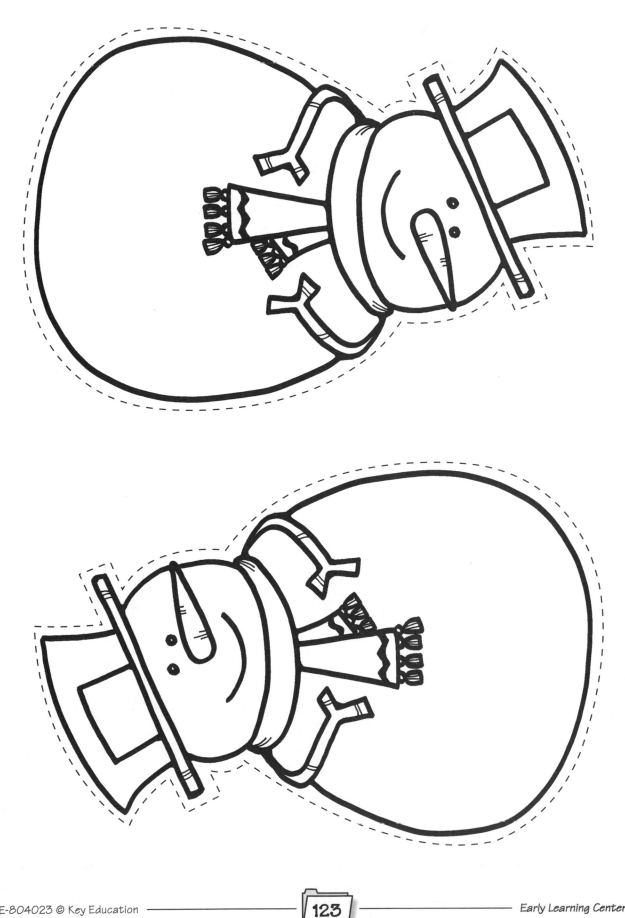

Flower Garden

Themes: Spring, Growing things

Skill: Number recognition, Sets

Preparation:

1. Make one copy of the flowerpot patterns (page 125). Color the pots as desired and cut out along the dashed lines. Laminate each flowerpot separately and trim.

2. Make one copy of the flower patterns (page 126). Color the flowers as desired and cut out along the dashed lines. Laminate each flower separately and trim.

Assembly:

1. Glue the flowerpots to the inside of a file folder as shown above. Glue only along the bottom and side edges of each pot, leaving the top free.

2. Attach the file folder name tag and the "To Play" instruction box on the outside of the file folder as shown on page 5.

3. Laminate the entire file folder. Trim around the edges.

4. Using a craft knife, carefully cut a slit through the laminate along the top of each flowerpot to create a pocket. Be sure not to cut through the file folder itself.

5. Place the laminated flowers in a quart-sized plastic zippered bag. Label the bag with a name tag and attach to the front of the file folder.

To Play:

- Place each flower in the correct flowerpot by matching the numeral on the pot to the number of dots on the flower.

- Have a friend check your work.

- Remove the flowers and put them back in the bag when you are finished.

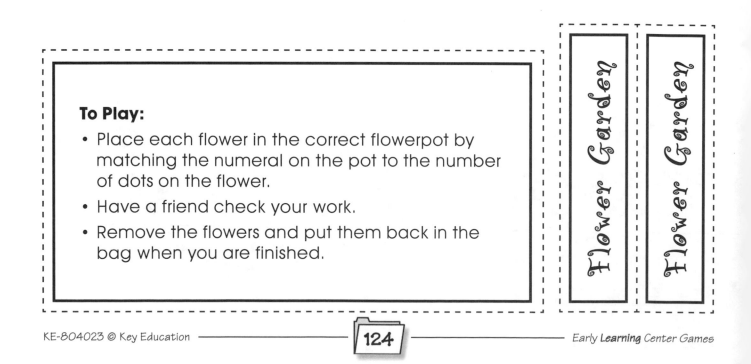

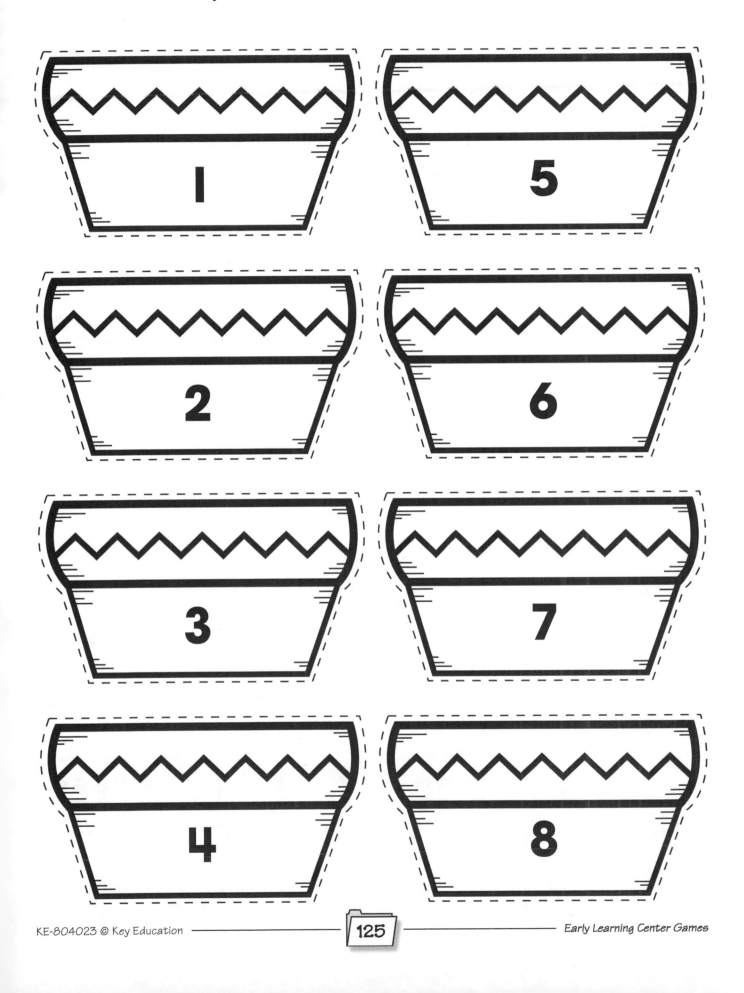

At the Beach

Themes: Summer, Ocean

Skill: Counting, Number recognition

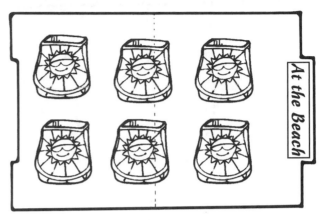

Preparation:

1. Make three copies of the beach bag patterns (page 128). Color as desired and cut out each bag along the dashed line. Write a number from 5 to 10 in the small square on each bag. (You may wish to do this AFTER the folder has been laminated so that the numbers on the bags can be changed.)

2. Make two copies of the beach item patterns (page 129). Color as desired and cut out the items along the dashed lines. Laminate each object separately and trim.

Assembly:

1. Glue the six beach bags to the inside of a file folder as shown above.

2. Attach the file folder name tag and the "To Play" instruction box on the outside of the file folder as shown on page 5.

3. Laminate the entire file folder. Trim around the edges.

4. Place all of the beach objects and a small ball of sticky-tack adhesive in a quart-sized plastic zippered bag. Label the bag with a name tag and attach to the front of the file folder.

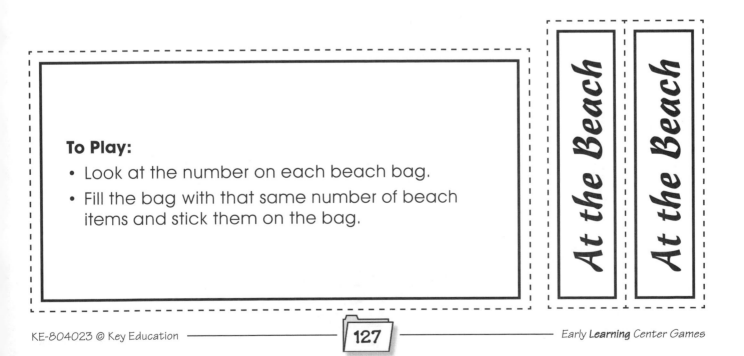

To Play:
- Look at the number on each beach bag.
- Fill the bag with that same number of beach items and stick them on the bag.

At the Beach

At the Beach

Autumn

Theme: Seasons

Skills: One-to-one correspondence, Drawing lines

Preparation:

1. Make two copies of the scarecrow patterns (page 131). Color as desired. Cut out the scarecrows along the dashed lines.
2. Make one copy of the crows pattern (page 132). Color as desired. Cut out the crows along the dashed lines.

Assembly:

1. Glue the 12 scarecrows randomly to the inside of a file folder as shown above.
2. Glue the 12 crows randomly to the folder as shown.
3. Attach the file folder name tag and the "To Play" instruction box on the outside of the file folder as shown on page 5.
4. Laminate the entire file folder. Trim around the edges.
5. Place several washable or dry-erase markers in a quart-sized plastic zippered bag. Label the bag with a name tag and attach to the front of the file folder.

To Play:

- Look at the scarecrows and the crows.
- Using a washable or dry-erase marker, draw a line from each scarecrow to the nearest crow.

Autumn

Autumn

Valentines

Theme: Valentine's Day

Skills: Counting, Following directions

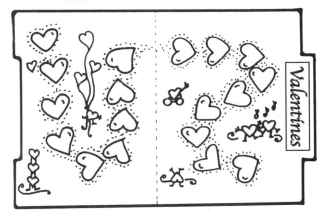

Preparation:

1. Make one copy of both of the heart game board patterns (pages 134–135). Color as desired. Cut out the game boards along the dashed lines and then trim around the game path.

2. Make one copy of the heart game cards (page 136). Color the cards as desired and cut apart along the dashed lines. Laminate each card separately and trim.

Assembly:

1. Glue the game board to the inside of a file folder as shown above by lining up the dashed edges at the center fold.

2. Attach the file folder name tag and the "To Play" instruction box on the outside of the file folder as shown on page 5.

3. Laminate the entire file folder. Trim around the edges.

4. Gather four small objects (e.g., erasers, small plastic figures, etc.) to use as game tokens to move around the board. Place the game tokens and heart game cards in a quart-sized plastic zippered bag. Label the bag with a name tag and attach to the front of the file folder.

To Play:

- Select a game token and place it on the space labeled "START."

- Draw one card. Move your game token the same number of spaces as indicated on the card. If there are instructions on the space where you land, follow the directions before finishing your turn.

- The first player to reach "Stop" wins!

Valentines

Start

Go ↑ 1 ♡

Go ↓ 1 ♡

Go → 2 ♡'s

Go →
2 ♡'s

Go ↗ 1 ♡

Go ↗ 1 ♡

Go → 1 ♡

End

Lucky Leprechauns

Theme: St. Patrick's Day

Skills: Number recognition, Counting, Number operations

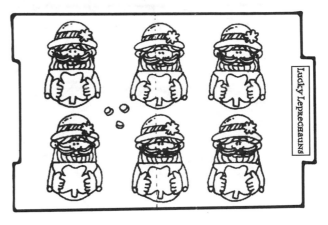

Preparation:

1. Make two copies of the lucky leprechaun patterns (page 138). Color as desired and cut out along the dashed lines. Laminate each leprechaun separately and trim.

2. Make four copies of the gold coin patterns (page 139) on goldenrod-colored paper. Cut out the coins. Laminate each coin separately and trim.

Assembly:

1. Glue the six laminated leprechauns to the inside of a file folder as shown above. Glue only around the edges and 1" (25 mm) below the dashed line on the pot of gold.

2. Attach the file folder name tag and the "To Play" instruction box on the outside of the file folder as shown on page 5.

3. Laminate the entire file folder. Trim around the edges.

4. Use a craft knife to cut pockets in the pots of gold. Carefully cut through the laminate and each pot of gold along the dashed line. Be sure not to cut through the file folder itself.

5. Place all of the coins in a plastic zippered sandwich bag. Label the bag with a name tag and attach to the front of the file folder.

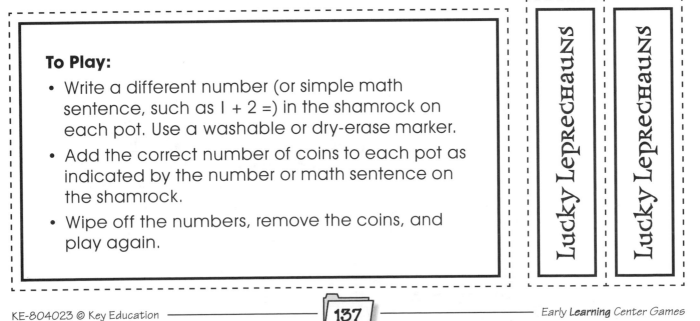

To Play:
- Write a different number (or simple math sentence, such as 1 + 2 =) in the shamrock on each pot. Use a washable or dry-erase marker.
- Add the correct number of coins to each pot as indicated by the number or math sentence on the shamrock.
- Wipe off the numbers, remove the coins, and play again.

Lucky Leprechauns

Lucky Leprechauns

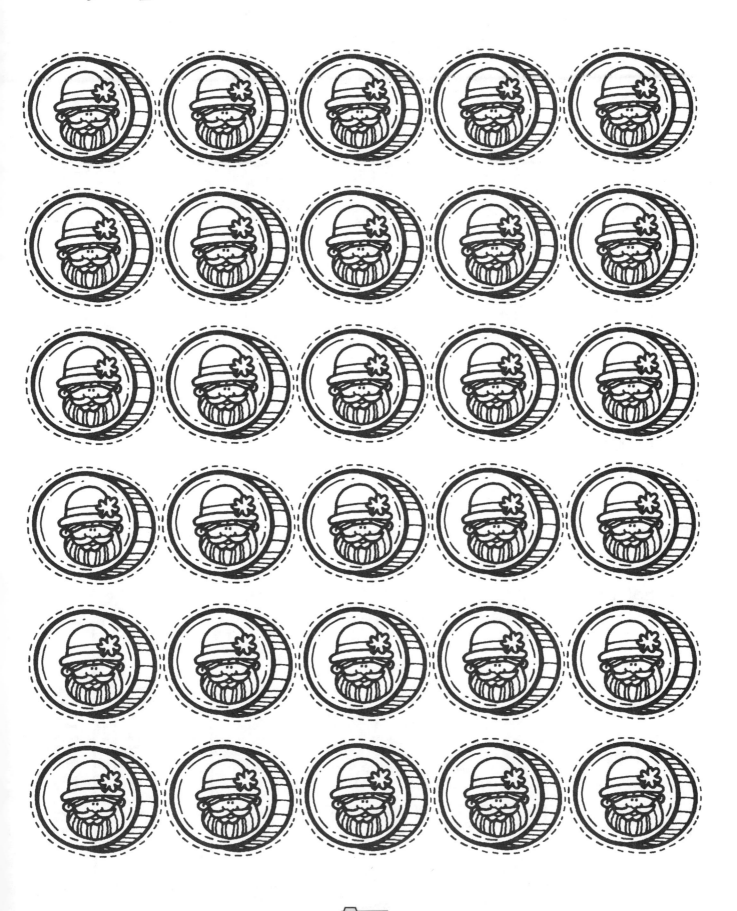

EGG HUNT

Theme: Easter/Spring

Skill: Matching, Sorting

Preparation:

1. Make three copies of the basket patterns (page 141). Color the baskets as desired and cut out along the solid black lines. Laminate each basket separately and trim.

2. Make six copies of the egg patterns (page 142). Color the six pages so that they are identical. Cut out the eggs along the dashed lines. Laminate each egg separately and trim.

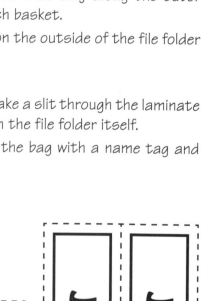

Assembly:

1. Glue the six baskets to the inside of a file folder as shown above. Glue only along the outer edges—do not put glue in the space 1½" from the top edge of each basket.

2. Attach the file folder name tag and the "To Play" instruction box on the outside of the file folder as shown on page 5.

3. Laminate the entire file folder. Trim around the edges.

4. Use a craft knife to cut pockets in the Easter baskets. Carefully make a slit through the laminate and each basket along the dashed line. Be sure not to cut through the file folder itself.

5. Place all of the eggs in a quart-sized plastic zippered bag. Label the bag with a name tag and attach to the front of the file folder.

Extension:

Extend the activity by supplying several blank or uncolored eggs. Have the children create more eggs to match those in the baskets.

To Play:

- Remove all of the Easter eggs from the bag.
- Sort the eggs into the Easter baskets so that all of the eggs in each basket are the same.

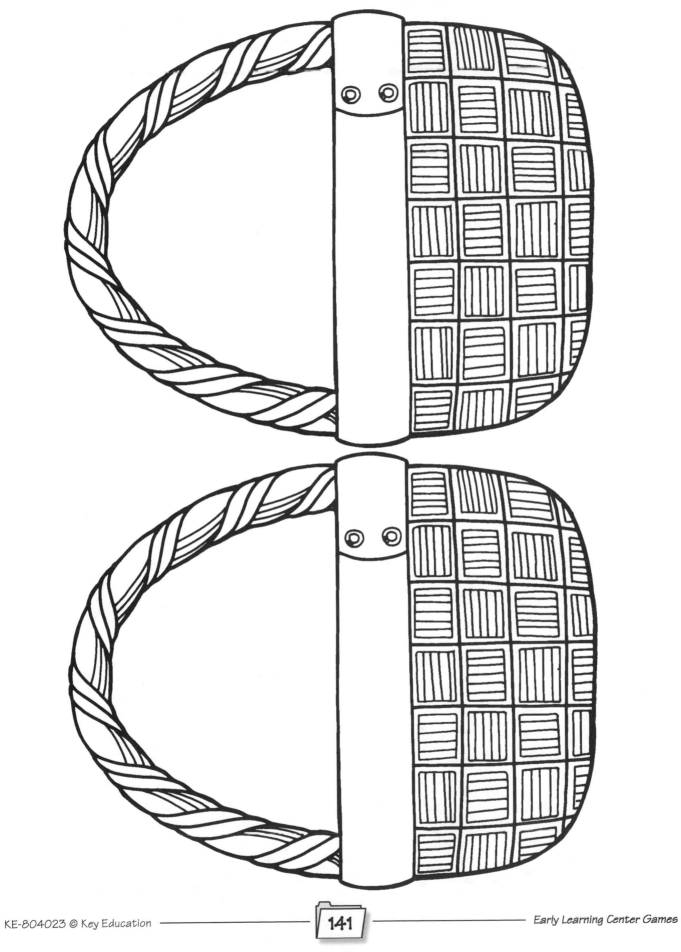

EGG HUNT

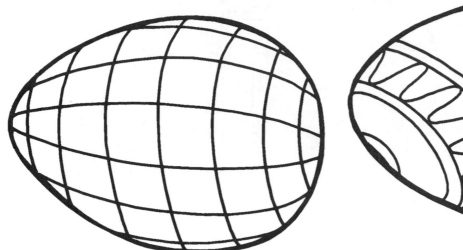

FIRECRACKERS AND FLAGS

Theme: Fourth of July

Skill: Building puzzles

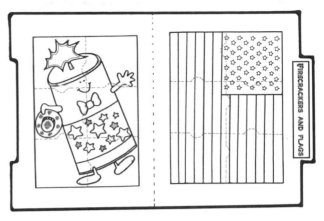

Preparation:

1. Make two copies of the firecracker (page 144) and 2 copies of either the American or Canadian flag puzzle patterns (pages 145-146). Color each set of pages so that they are identical. Cut out each pattern along the dashed line. Set aside one copy of each pattern.

2. Cut apart the second copy of the firecracker and flag patterns along the dashed lines to create puzzle pieces. Write a number 1 on the back of each piece of the firecracker puzzle and a number 2 on each piece of the flag puzzle. Laminate each piece separately and trim.

Assembly:

1. Glue the complete firecracker pattern on the left-hand side of the file folder. Glue the complete flag (American or Canadian) pattern to the right-hand side as shown above.

2. Attach the file folder name tag and the "To Play" instruction box on the outside of the file folder as shown on page 5.

3. Laminate the entire file folder. Trim around the edges.

4. Place the firework and flag puzzle pieces in two separate plastic zippered sandwich bags. Label each bag with a name tag and attach to the front of the file folder.

To Play:

- Look at the puzzle guides inside the file folder.
- Match pieces to each guide to put together the firecracker and flag puzzles.

FIRECRACKERS AND FLAGS

FIRECRACKERS AND FLAGS

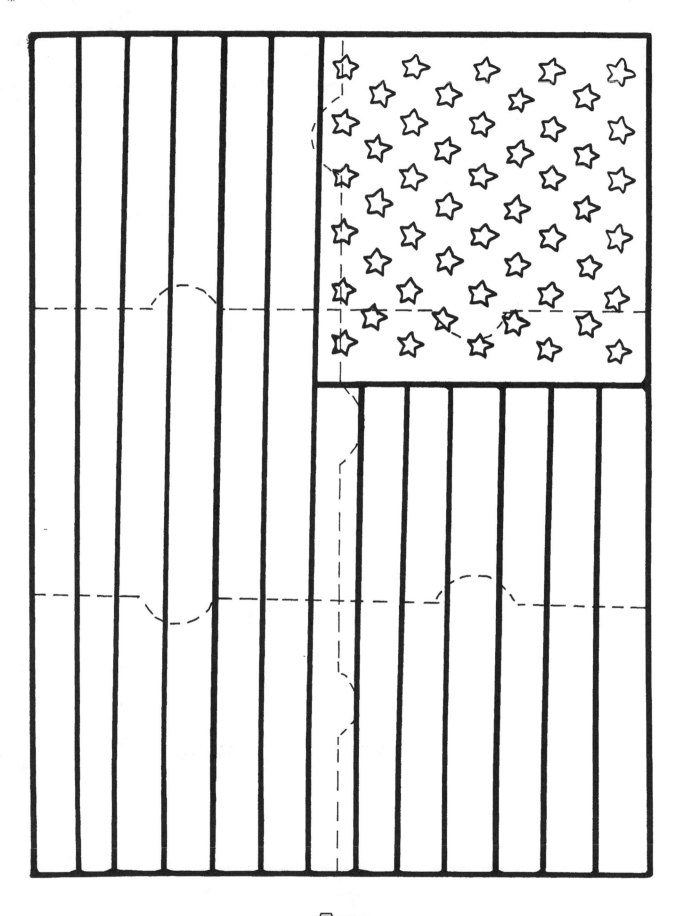

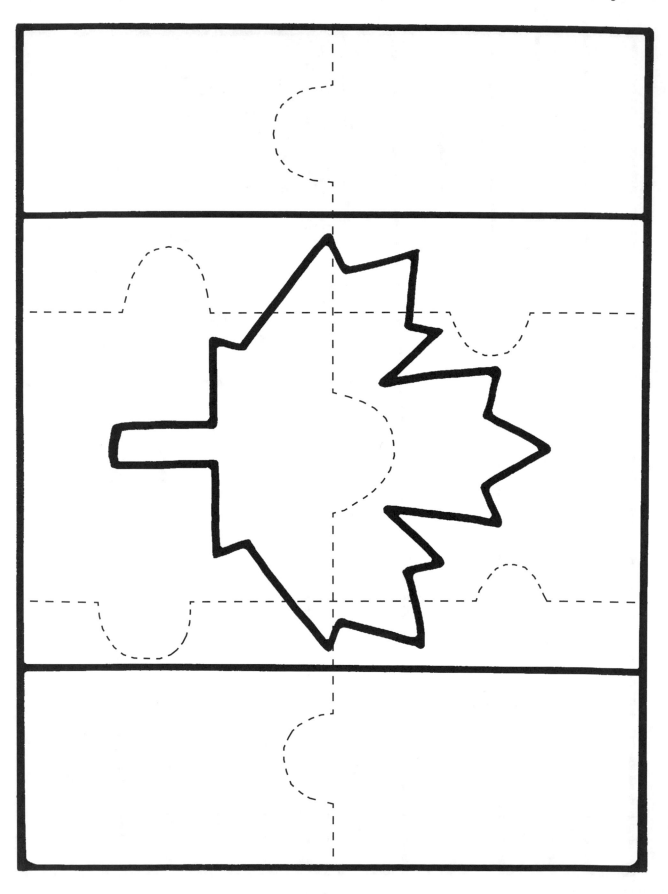

HALLOWEEN

Theme: Halloween

Skill: Sorting, Sequencing: large, medium, small

Preparation:

1. Make one copy each of the treat bag patterns (pages 148–149). Color as desired and cut out the bags along the dashed lines. Laminate each bag separately and trim.

2. Make one copy of each of the Halloween treat card patterns (pages 150–152). Color the items and cut apart the cards along the dashed lines. Laminate each treat card separately and trim.

Assembly:

1. Glue the three laminated bags to the inside of a file folder in descending order of size as shown above. Glue only along the bottom and side edges of each bag, leaving the top free of glue.

2. Attach the file folder name tag and the "To Play" instruction box on the outside of the file folder as shown on page 5.

3. Laminate the entire file folder. Trim around the edges.

4. Use a craft knife to cut pockets in the treat bags. Carefully cut through the laminate along the top of each bag. Be sure not to cut through the file folder itself.

5. Place all of the treats in a quart-sized plastic zippered bag. Label the bag with a name tag and attach to the front of the file folder.

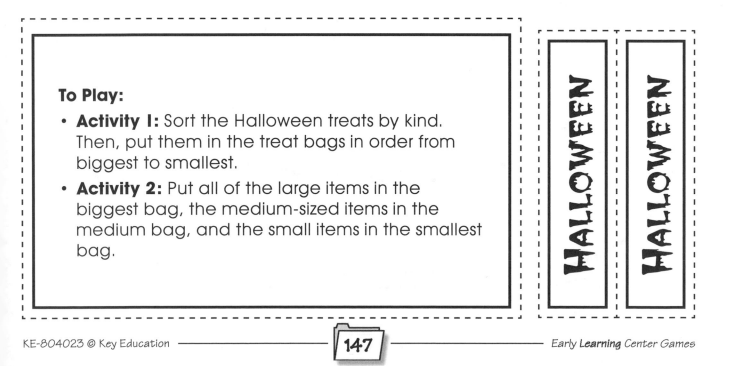

To Play:

- **Activity I:** Sort the Halloween treats by kind. Then, put them in the treat bags in order from biggest to smallest.

- **Activity 2:** Put all of the large items in the biggest bag, the medium-sized items in the medium bag, and the small items in the smallest bag.

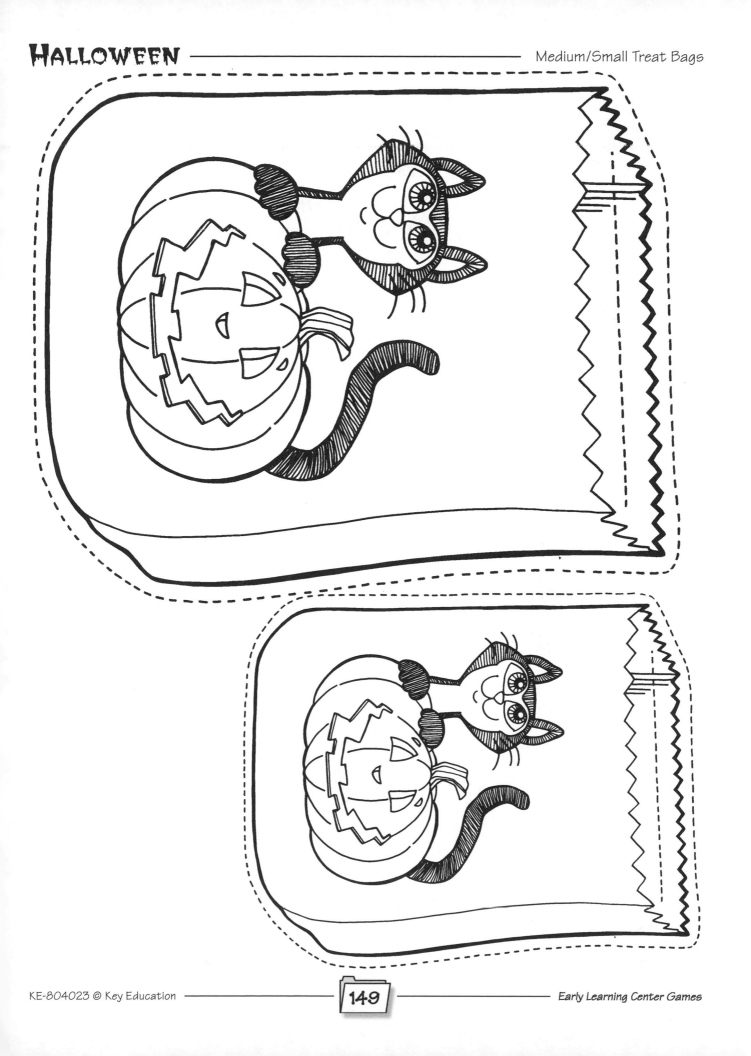

149

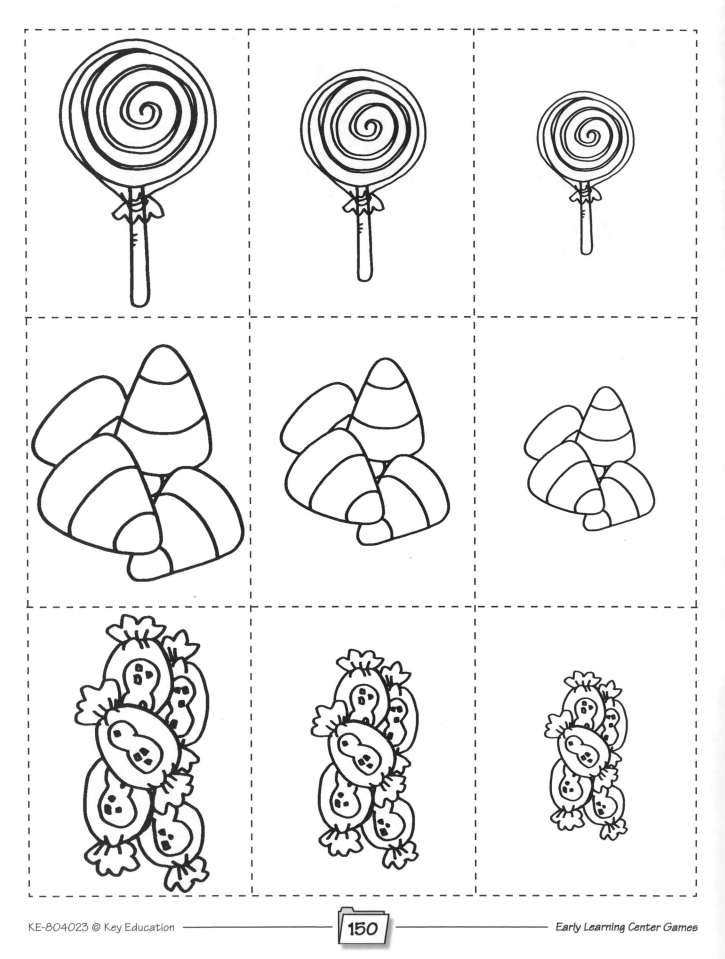

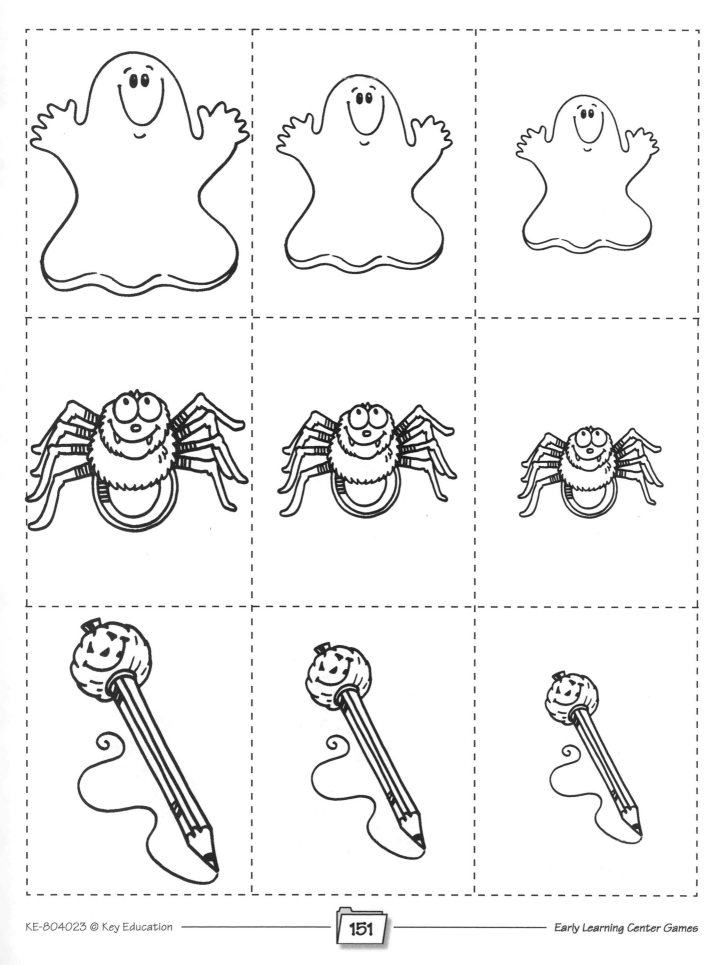

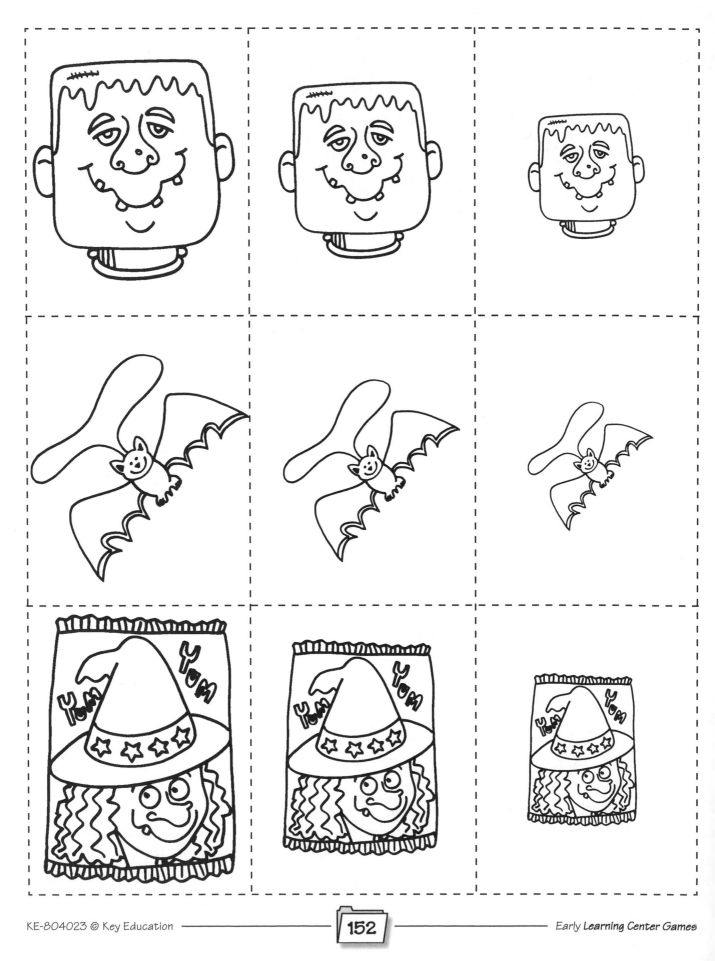

Thanksgiving

Theme: Thanksgiving

Skill: Patterning

Preparation:

1. Make twelve copies of the Thanksgiving figure patterns (below). Color as desired and cut out the figures along the dashed lines. Laminate each piece separately and trim.

2. Make one copy of the Thanksgiving pattern cards (page 154). Color as desired and cut apart the cards along the dashed lines.

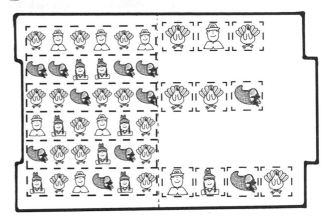

Assembly:

1. Glue the Thanksgiving pattern cards to the inside of a file folder as shown above.

2. Attach the file folder name tag and the "To Play" instruction box on the outside of the file folder as shown on page 5.

3. Laminate the entire file folder. Trim around the edges.

4. Place all of the Thanksgiving figures and a small ball of sticky-tack adhesive in a quart-sized plastic zippered bag. Label the bag with a name tag and attach to the front of the file folder.

To Play:

- Continue each pattern.
- Find the correct Thanksgiving figures and stick them to the folder in the correct order.

Thanksgiving

Thanksgiving

Hanukkah

Theme: Hanukkah

Skill: Graphing

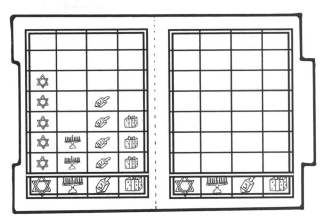

Preparation:

1. Make two or three copies of the Hanukkah card patterns (page 156). Color as desired and cut apart the cards along the dashed lines. Laminate each card separately and trim.

2. Make two copies of the Hanukkah grid pattern (page 157), one on colorful paper and the other on white paper.

Assembly:

1. Glue the colorful Hanukkah grid on the left-hand side of the file folder. Glue the white Hanukkah grid to the right-hand side of the file folder.

2. Attach the file folder name tag and the "To Play" instruction box on the outside of the file folder as shown on page 5.

3. Laminate the entire file folder. Trim around the edges.

4. Place the Hanukkah cards in four separate snack-sized plastic zippered bags—one bag per Hanukkah image. Put the four bags, one die, and a small ball of sticky-tack adhesive in a large plastic zippered bag. Label the bag with a name tag and attach to the front of the file folder.

To Play:

- Choose one set of Hanukkah cards. Roll the die and take that same number of cards from the bag.

- Using the sticky tack, attach the cards to the color grid in the column with the same icon.

- Using a washable or dry-erase marker, color in squares on the white grid to match the graph you created with the cards. (Example: If you rolled a 6 and put 6 "Star of David" cards on the color grid, then color 6 squares in the Star of David column on the white grid.)

- Choose a new set of cards and repeat.

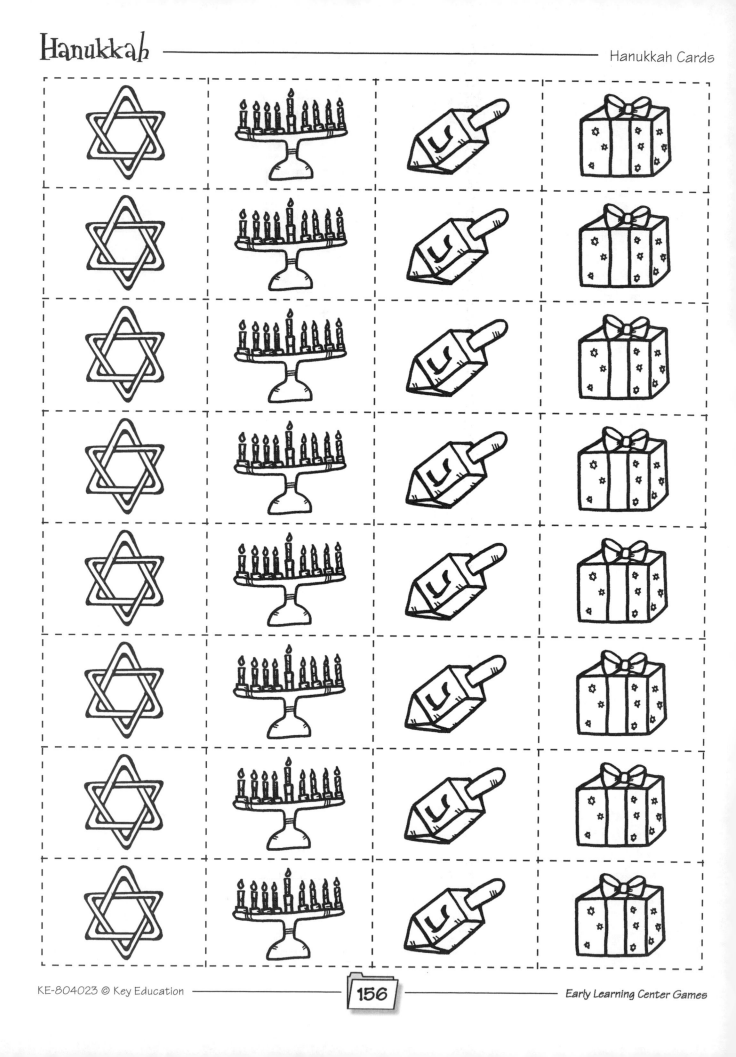

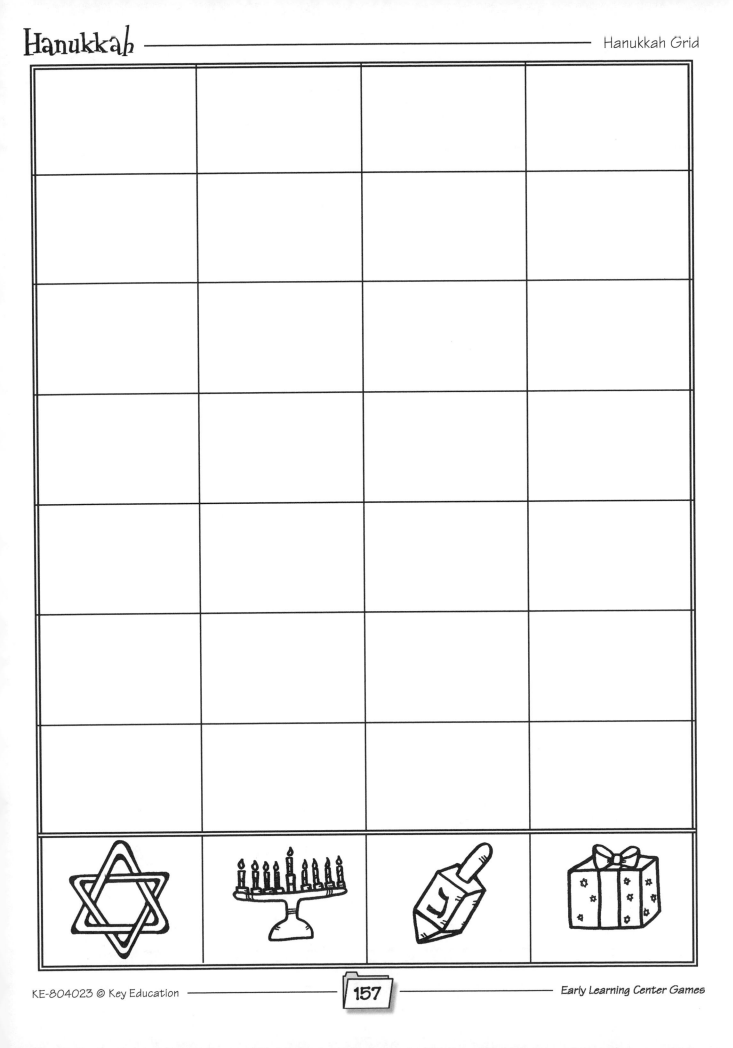

Gifts

Themes: Christmas, Hanukkah, Kwanzaa, Celebrations

Skills: Patterning, Drawing

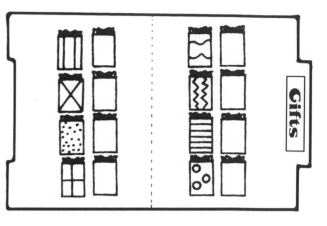

Preparation:

1. Make one copy of the assorted gift box patterns (page 159). Color the gifts as desired. Cut out the gifts along the dashed lines.
2. Make one copy of the blank gift box patterns (page 160). Cut out the gifts along the dashed lines.

Assembly:

1. Glue the patterned gifts to the inside of a file folder as shown above. Glue the blank gifts next to the patterned gifts.
2. Attach the file folder name tag and the "To Play" instruction box on the outside of the file folder as shown on page 5.
3. Laminate the entire file folder. Trim around the edges.
4. Place an assortment of washable or dry-erase markers in a zippered plastic sandwich bag. Label the bag with a name tag and attach to the front of the file folder.

Extension:

Make copies of the blank gift box patterns (page 160) and have the children create their own gifts for one another to duplicate.

To Play:
- Look at each patterned gift box.
- Using the pattern as a guide, color the blank gift box to the right so that it looks the same.

Gifts

Gifts

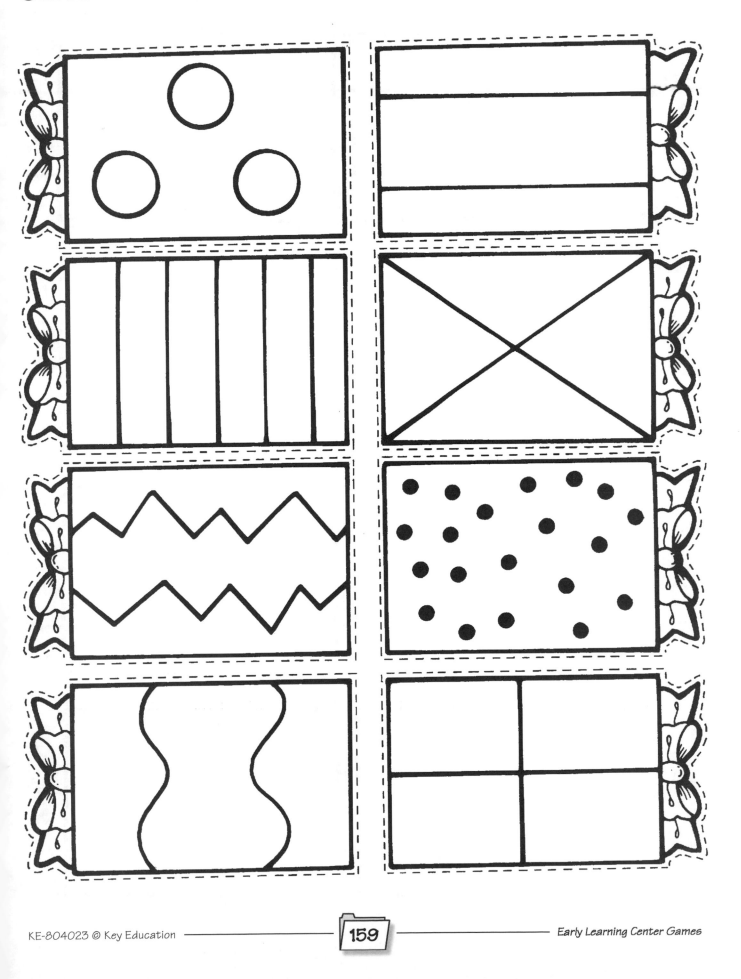

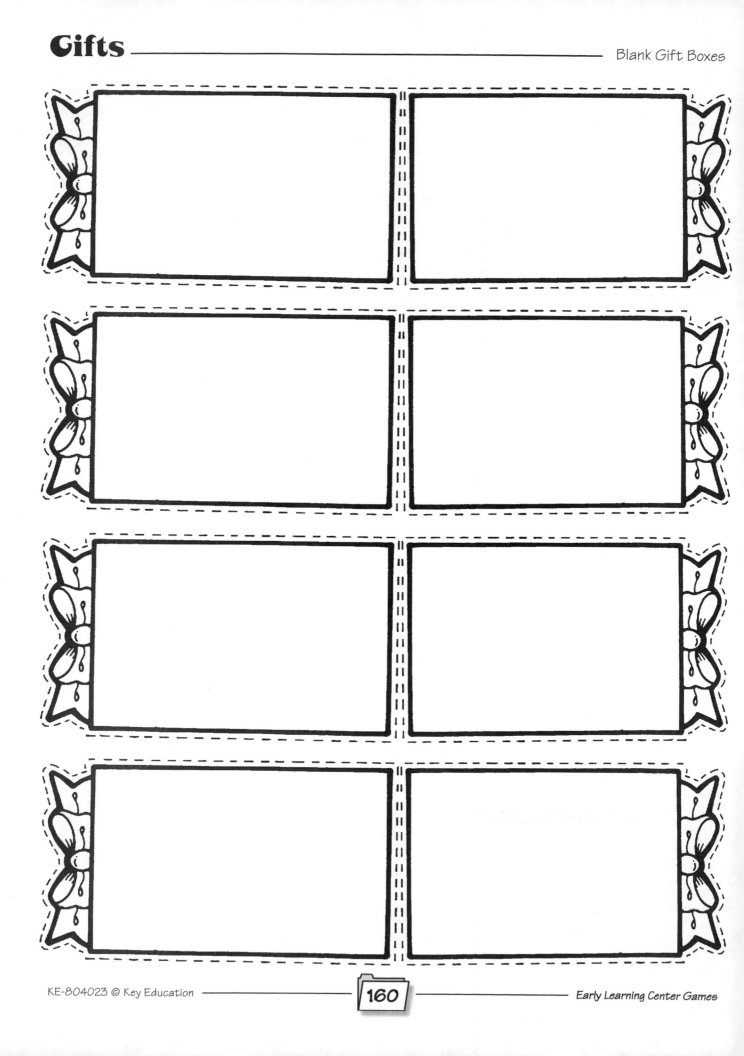